ET CETERA, ET CETERA

Ruth Majkau

Things I need to buy
- Tampons 5$
- Toilet paper 5$
- plastic plates 3$

TO DO -
- clean out car
- clean house
- write paper / mom
- give to mom
- ask mom for $ for

BY LEWIS THOMAS

The Lives of a Cell
The Medusa and the Snail
The Youngest Science
Late Night Thoughts on Listening to
Mahler's Ninth Symphony
Et Cetera, Et Cetera

ET CETERA, ET CETERA

Notes of a Word-Watcher

by

LEWIS THOMAS

Welcome Rain Publishers · New York

ET CETERA, ET CETERA:
Notes of a Word-Watcher
First Welcome Rain edition 2000
Printed in Canada.

Direct any inquiries to
Welcome Rain Publishers LLC,
225 West 35th Street,
Suite 1100, New York, NY 10001.

ISBN 1-56649-166-5
Manufactured in Canada
by BLAZE I.P.I.

First Edition: July 2000
3 5 7 9 10 8 6 4 2

Contents

ET CETERA,
ET CETERA

Introduction

As far back as I can remember, dictionaries have been part of the furniture in our house. I have had the American Heritage Dictionary propped against one leg of my easy chair, and a heavy etymology book, usually Barnhart, against the other, and Pokorny's *Indogermanisches Etymologisches Wörterbuch* within easy reach on a shelf alongside. The AHD is still the 1969 edition, on the rug for nearly twenty years, and before that it was Webster. My wife isn't sure she trusts these sources, preferring the Oxford English Dictionary, all the volumes on another shelf where she can get to them whenever disputes arise, as they do.

An instance, What about DELIGHT? one of us asked, a while back, setting both of us in motion, interrupting whatever we happened to be reading or looking at on television.

DELIGHT seems, for reasons that are obvious on the face of it, one of the lightest words in the language, an airy breath of a word, all pleasure, luminous, lit from within.

But there is no lasting light in *delight;* its cognates carry soft warnings of the shadow just ahead. It is a transient word, here now, gone in a minute, nice while it lasts, maybe hard to remember clearly moments later. Some of the cognates, from the Latin *delectare,* to charm, allure, and *delicatus,* luxurious, dainty, and Late Latin *deliciosus,* tell us what to expect in delight, but leave us with the sense that whatever it was, however delightful, delicious, dainty and delicate, it most likely won't last long. Niagara Falls, said Gertrude Stein, is beautiful for thirty seconds.

The foreboding in delight comes from the Indo-European root — nothing at all to do with light, plain old IE *lek,* meaning a cord, a snag, a lure. Pokorny (p. 673) produces a committee of German synonyms: *fangen,* to capture, *reizen,* to taste, to charm. But only in Latin do the real cognates turn up: *delecto, lacto,* connected to allurement, seduction, teasing. Nothing about light, all about the pleasure of being ensnared. Delight is a moment of pleasure, take it while you have it; don't wait, don't look ahead.

Sober light is something else, too serious for such light meaning. *Leuk* was the IE root, leading to LUCID, ILLUMINATE, LUNAR, important matters, not there just for fun. *Leghwu* was the root meaning light in weight, some fun there in LEVITY, but no link between this sense of light and the slightly sinful, flickering DELIGHT.

And so, in this manner, lists of words and more words

about words began to grow into stacks like furniture, hence this book.

As I hope will become clear, but perhaps not too blindingly clear, this book is not at all a scholarly work. I have relied on secondary publications for whatever information I have used, standard dictionaries and etymological glossaries available everywhere; I have spent no time in library stacks discovering original sources. My sole qualification for writing these essays on (mostly) Indo-European roots is that I've been enchanted and obsessed by them for over twenty years, and have convinced myself that these antique words continue to hold their old meaning long after almost vanishing into the words of modern English.

I am happy to acknowledge an obligation to the Cornell University College of Medicine, and to Dean Tom Shires, for providing office facilities and the lofty faculty title of Scholar-in-Residence, making the task of writing seem not only possible but mandatory. I am grateful to my wife, Beryl, for many of the ideas in the essays, and for her wise, gentle and exceedingly firm editorial judgment throughout the writing. My daughter Abigail bears the responsibility for starting me off on the book in the first place, and she and Chuck Verrill helped in many ways. Liz Darhansoff guided the enterprise along, seeing to it that it got finished. It is a nice piece of luck to have had the manuscript scrutinized and edited by Irv Goodman and his colleagues. And my special thanks to my assistant, Stephanie Hemmert, who has typed, stored, retrieved and sometimes exhumed one draft after another, with abiding patience and skill.

Chapter 40 (Testament, Third Party, Gaia etc.) is adapted, with the publisher's permission, from an essay in the book *Living Philosophies*, edited by Clifton Fadiman, published by Doubleday. The same essay appears in the Summer Edition of Grand Street magazine.

1

———

ANIMUS, AGE etc.

In our backyard is a horse-chestnut tree the size of a church. It is said to be two hundred years old, it is about one hundred twenty feet high, at its base the circumference of the trunk is almost twenty-five feet. Its limbs are the size of telephone poles but somehow flexible, extending straight out from the trunk as the most improbable things on earth, then sloping to the ground thirty feet out and rising again to nearly their original level.

Bare-naked in winter, leafless, it somehow looks as energetically alive as when full-leaved in high summer. When I am standing under it on the moss, looking up through the columns and leaves, it has a church-like feel, and it is so quiet that it startles.

I am not an animist. I am an accredited twentieth-century scientist, but I swear to you that that tree is inhabited.

It is easier to think and say something like that, for a scientist today, without attracting sidelong looks or

———

7

Et Cetera, Et Cetera

being put away for a time of counseling. It does indeed
have a spirit inside, but we have covered that feeling by
an antique phrase, "the genius of the place." We do not
come right out and say that it is numinous, that it pos-
sesses a power, its *numen;* it rarely crosses our mind that
these words come to us from the Indo-European root
neu, meaning simply a NOD, now a divine NOD, both
assent and command.

If I were an early, primitive man, instead of the late
man that I feel these days, and if I had not yet built a
language for naming my tree, dumbstruck, I would go
looking for a small child. What is it, I would ask. The
child would say a word never heard before, pointing up
into the tree in eagerness for my attention. The word
would have the sound of *ai,* then a gentle breath, *aiw,*
and it would sound right for this tree. The word would
then enter the language by way of me, I would tell it to
my friends, and thousands of generations later, long
after my time, it would be used to describe many things,
not trees but the *feeling* that was contained in that particular tree. *Aiw* would become EVER, and AYE, and
EON and AGE. The Sanskrit language would have built
it into the word *ayua,* meaning life. Gothic would have
used it for a word, *aiwos,* eternity. Latin would have
placed it in *aevem* and *aetas,* for the connected ideas of
age and eternity. The Greeks would put it into *aion,*
vital force, and we would receive it in our word EON.
German would have it as *ewig,* the word sung over and
over by a high voice in Mahler's *Das Lied von der Erde.*
And some of the languages, in their hopes, would insert
a *yeu* sound as a prefix, and the new sound would form

Animus, Age etc.

words for YOUTH, YOUNG, JUVENILE. By this time all traces of meaning of the chestnut tree would be gone.

In order to get a language really to work from the outset, as a means of human communication by speech, it must have been technically obligatory to make, first off, the words needed to express the feelings aroused by things, particularly living things in the world. Naming as a taxonomic problem could come later and would take care of itself. But for ideas to begin flowing in and out of minds, so that the deepest indispensability of language could take hold, the feelings would have to come first into speech, and that sense of the roots must persist like genes in all the words to follow.

I notice a squirrel as he leaps from one outer branch to another on a limb high up in the sunshine of my chestnut tree. I have as yet no name for such a thing, so I turn to the small child at my side, and point. He looks carefully, thinks for a moment, then says *an-e*, two light syllables, sure of his word. So I name the squirrel by that word and my friends and neighbors agree, and the name moves into the new language, but only for a while as *this* name. After only a few generations, our progeny have devised a new, more accurate and specific name for the squirrel, taking it from a root indicating the most conspicuous feature of the creature, its great tail resembling a shadow. So the squirrel became, literally, the shadow-tailed, *skiouros* (*skia*, shadow, plus *oura*, tail), and English turned this to SQUIRREL.

And what happened to the child's name, *an-e*? All sorts of things, holding it in each IE language with the first feeling still in place. The child's sharp sense of the

new object, there in the great tree, was that *it breathes*
and is *alive,* and *an-e* became the source of Sanskrit
aniti, he breathes, and Greek *anemos,* wind, breath, and
Latin *anima,* life, breath, and for us ANIMATE, ANIMAL
and ANIMUS. ANEMONE. And when we have in mind
one of our own qualities, setting us loose in high spirits,
MAGNANIMITY.

2

SEW, BEAR, BROTHER, DEW etc.

Indo-European is the scholarly, nineteenth-century name for a language presumed to have been spoken some thousands of years ago, nobody knows how many thousands. Whenever, it was the parent of almost all the languages now spoken in the Western World: Latin, Greek, Sanskrit, German, French, Spanish, Italian, all the Slavic languages, every European tongue except Magyar and Basque. Its offspring include Old Persian and modern Iranian, Hittite, and Tocharian (a language spoken long ago in part of western China). The scholarship on which Indo-European philology is based had its beginnings in 1786, at a meeting of the Asiatic Society in Calcutta, when Sir William Jones, an English jurist and amateur student of classical linguistics, pointed out that

the Sanskrit language, whatever be its antiquity, is of a wonderful structure: more perfect than the

Et Cetera, Et Cetera

Greek, more copious than the Latin, and more ex-
quisitely refined than either, yet bearing to both
of them a stronger affinity, both in the roots of
verbs and in the forms of grammar, than could
possibly have been produced by accident: so
strong, indeed, that no philologer could examine
them all three, without believing them to have
sprung from some common source, which, perhaps, no longer exists.

It is a rather sad footnote in linguistic history that
another Englishman, James Parsons, just missed his
chance at the scholarly immortality now attributed to
Sir William Jones. Parsons, a physician and fellow of
both the Royal Society and the Society of Antiquaries,
had arrived at much the same conclusion as Jones
twenty years earlier, and on much the same body of evidence. In 1767 he published *The Remains of Japhet,
Being Historical Enquiries Into the Affinity and Origins
of the European Languages.* In this long and regrettably
tedious book, Parsons laid out the similarities among
words in English, Irish, Welsh, Greek, Italic, Germanic,
Slavic and Iranian, and proposed a common ancestral
language for the whole group. His mistake was to become inextricably entangled in scriptural disputations,
centering his discovery on the contention that the first
language was that of Noah's third son Japhet, whose
offspring carried it abroad from Armenia, the resting
place of the Ark. Nobody seems to have wished to follow
the argument, and Parson's excellent work remained in
obscurity.

Sew, Bear, Brother, Dew etc.

Jones was long neglected as well, but about forty years later his 1786 paper was picked up and run with by several generations of German linguists, starting with Franz Bopp and followed by eminent scores of comparative philologists, including the versatile Jacob Grimm and his brother. Everything, or nearly everything, was sorted out. The sentus-kentus dichotomy seemed to be settled — all of Roman Europe said *k*entus, while all the Eastern neighbors said *s*entus (but later, to everyone's confusion, Tocharian, farthest east, turned out to be saying kentus). Anyway, most of the rest fell neatly into place. There was, by all the evidence, a common language spoken by the Celts throughout Britain and Ireland, using words and grammar similar to those spoken in Iran and India, and many of these resemble to a startling degree the elements of today's perfect English. Indeed, Eire and Iran, for all their different populations, are cognate names, taken from the same ancestral tongue, along with Aryan.

The basic method for setting about the process of comparative philology consists of locating as many closely related words as can be found in the Indo-European family of languages, and then deducing from their structure the form of the original ancestral word. The result is necessarily hypothetical, but the evidence supporting the guess at the root is usually persuasive. The English word s ew provides a nice example of the method at work. There are records in Middle English of a word *seuwen*, and an earlier word in Old English *siwian*, meaning to stitch with needle and thread. Still earlier, similar terms were identified in Old Frisian *sia*,

Old High German *siuwen*, Old Icelandic *syja*, Gothic *siujan*, and Latin had *suo*, *suere*, to sew. Hittite had *sumanza*, a thread or cord. Old Slavic contained *siti*, Lithuanian *siuti*, and Sanskrit *sivyati*, he sews, and *syuman*, a suture. The Sanskrit *sutra* originally meant a string or thread; thus the *Kama Sutra* was a long string of aphorisms and rules concerning love.

On the basis of this and other words related to sewing, dug out of one ancient language after another, the nineteenth-century scholars concluded that there must have been a parent word in the proto–Indo-European language, in the form of *syewa* or *sewa*, the earliest ancestor of SEW.

Despite the distance of time, many of the Indo-European words in everyday use six thousand or more years ago are surprisingly similar to their remote descendants in modern English, looking and sounding much like the same words spoken with a heavy foreign accent. A *bher* was a BEAR, *bhrater* was a BROTHER, *dheu* was DEW, *dwer* a DOOR, *gno* KNOW, *man* MAN, *nepot* a NEPHEW, *nizdo* a bird's NEST. *Spyeu* was to SPIT, also SPUTTER and SPEW. To *wen* was to WIN, to *trem* was to TREMBLE. *Wokso* was WAX, *wopsa* a WASP, a *yero* a YEAR. Wonderfully, *yek* was a JOKE.

Moreover, the similarities seem to have hung on in each of the languages that intervene between that ancient tongue, the oldest of which we have any solid knowledge, and today's English. The most ordinary words keep reappearing, shaped and sounded differently but always retaining, often tucked away inside, a strange sort of family resemblance.

Sew, Bear, Brother, Dew etc.

Pick a word, any word — "it" for instance. Such a simple word as IT was *ko* in Indo-European, with a variant *ki*, the indispensable stem of a pronoun meaning, generally, "this." From this root came germanic *hi*, evolving into Old English as *hit*, IT, HE, HIM and HIS. In fact, the *ke* in *ke-etero*, "this remains," appears to be the origin of ET CETERA.

Oino was the IE root for ONE; suffixed as *oiniko*, it served for later words meaning "any," including Old High German *einag*, Old Frisian *enig*, Old Icelandic *einigr*, Old English *aenig*, and English ANY. Our sparse word for ourselves, "us," is tracked back to IE *nes*, the root for first person plural pronouns, with intervening words *uns* in Germanic, *nos* Latin, *nas* Sanskrit, *nas* Hittite, *ny* Welsh, *oss* Old Icelandic, finally English US.

I first encountered a lexicon of these wild old words, some of them like grenade fragments of words, about twenty years ago in the 1969 edition of the American Heritage Dictionary, and became hooked immediately. The volume, which I still have at hand, contains a scholarly section by Professor Calvert Watkins of Harvard, describing the methods and conclusions arrived at in comparative philology over two centuries of research. Although my days and most evenings at the time were spent in a microbiology laboratory, busy with other details, I became convinced that the accomplishments of comparative philology were as exacting, quantitative and predictive as those of any other science I'd looked at, despite its conventional segregation among the academic humanities. The more I read about it, as an outsider, the more I came to believe that of all the fields in biology, this one was the most directly and specifically connected to human biology. The mark of being human is speech and the ready use of metaphor, and the evolutionary development of this trait is told, in part, by the history of words. So, as an outsider, an unschooled amateur, I have for fifteen years been looking over the shoulders of the scientists engaged in this work. My wife presented me some years ago with the 1969 edition of Julius Pokorny's *Indogermanisches Etymologisches Wörterbuch*, and with the help of an old German-English pocket dictionary I began to lose all spare time. I am, of course, not finished, nor am I ever sure I've really *learned* much; I keep forgetting words. But forgetting is part of the fun, allowing the pleasure of looking them up and being flabbergasted all over again.

I should confess that in all these twenty years I've stayed a careful distance from the field of proper, contemporary linguistics. Saussure, Heidegger, Chomsky and their successors, having changed forever the concerns of modern philosophy, remain beyond my grasp, and I am still contentedly trapped in another century.

Instead of becoming an apprentice, training my mind to comprehend the modern science of linguistics, then perhaps to construct new hypotheses to account for the intricacies of grammar, I turned into an obsessed collector, picking up and storing in the untidy attic of my mind words upon words. I have them now in overspilling stacks, arranged in what began as a kind of order — good words, bad ones, hybrids and related outrages, ambiguities, words with thirty-six or more dark meanings lurking inside. I bought a tabletop computer with its printer spilling yards of paper across the floor of my study and began storing new lists of roots and progeny words, confident that when I had catalogued them all I would be able to press a set of keys and out would come, in a shower of my own words, the truth of language. Then, three years ago, the chimney of my house caught fire; it spread to other rooms, and the computer and printer were found next morning, melted and annealed to my desk, like an item of found art, a modern museum piece, and I went back to the notes scrawled on yellow pads.

Later on, I decided to give up the hope for a filing system of any complexity, and jumbled all my lists together under the heading "interesting" words. It was only then that I made what I now claim as my own discovery, my illumination, not a theory of language but a statement of plain fact: there are no *uninteresting* words, not in English, not in Indo-European, not (I have to guess here, because of sparse acquaintance) in any of the languages in between. Not, I happily predict, in any of the three thousand or more separate languages now spoken on the planet. Every word, no exceptions, is an enchantment, a wonder, a marvel. But still, some of them have relentlessly carried along, from generation to generation, what seem to my mind to be moral instructions, good for the species, and the longest list on my pads is an array of such words, aphorisms compressed to single words, sometimes single phonemes.

3

PESSIMISM, FEET etc.

We've always been pleased with ourselves for being a two-legged species, proud of this special gift of agility, getting around neatly on just our feet, also taking great pride in the moral metaphor of uprightness. Other species, lesser, need all four limbs for getting around; some of our cousins, baboons, chimps and gorillas, can manage our trick, but only part-time. We, in contrast, are *Homo erectus,* a mark of genetic distinction gratifying us almost as much as being *Homo sapiens sapiens.* That extra *sapiens* is on there because of taxonomic rules, but how pleasingly it rings in our minds. (Judicious, wise etc. — from *sap,* taste.) We allowed Neanderthal into our class as *Homo sapiens* (fire, a tool or two), but then added an extra *sapiens* for our splendid, savvy selves.

But the language has sent us, long since, warnings against reading too much into that *erectus.* Bipeds, watch your feet! the language says.

I was sleepless one night, worrying about one thing

---

or another, then one thing *and* another and then another, and the word *pessimism* slid sidewise into my mind. I recalled that there was something worrying in the word, then as always couldn't remember what, so I heaved into the other room to look it up.

There it was; *of course*, I told myself, knew it all the time. Then, as always, the surprise and shock — not shock of recognition, shock of realization. This is an old, familiar experience for me: looking up words whose roots I've seen over and over before, then being astonished; one slow take after another.

PESSIMISM comes to us from an IE root *ped*, meaning nothing more or less than FOOT.

One thing the language does for us is to make sure we retain a measure, maybe small for most of us, of humility. As soon as we had agreed on a word for FOOT, we set off on cognate words for the ways of getting things wrong with feet.

One of the earliest offspring of *ped* turned up in Sanskrit as *padyate*, he falls. *Ped* became *fot* in Germanic; English saw new possibilities for fallibility and made FOOTLESS and FOOTLING, both meaning graceless, stupid.

Ped came to Latin as the root of *pes, pedis*, producing words all feet in one form or another, from which we have taken PEDESTRIAN, PEDAL, PEDIGREE (a goose's foot), straightforward enough.

But because of the old human troubles with footwork, other darker metaphors emerged as cognates. Latin *impedere* had the meaning of shackles, from which we derive IMPEDE, and *pedica*, a snare or fetter, hence our

IMPEACH. EXPEDITE emerged from the meaning to free from shackles. When someone has been trying too hard to better his lot and gets it wrong, we say he shot himself in the foot; worse still for him if he happens to have, as also happens with such people, his foot in his mouth.

The lasting power of *ped* as a root with its own plans for the future is shown by the convergence of an old Germanic cognate with the same meaning as the Latin *pedica*, shackle. Old English took *fet* from *fot* to make *feter*, from which we have FETTER itself.

What about my insomnia word? From the IE compound *ped-samo*, something bad, Latin made *pessimus*, the worst of things, the superlative of *malus*, and we borrowed this to form PESSIMISM.

Putting a foot wrong shifts the root just a bit; *ped* becomes *ped-ko*, opening the way to Latin *peccare* to stumble, to sin, PECCABLE. Also an opening to one of the great learned puns of military history. The British general Sir Charles Napier (1782–1853), ordered to take command of the city of Sind in India, sent back a message after his success consisting of the solitary word *peccavi* (I have Sind).

Our uneasiness about our feet turns up in other words, scandal and slander for instance (q.v.); the language worries endlessly over getting its feet ensnared, trapped. We live in the apprehension of stumbling, literally over our feet and metaphorically over our words. The IE root for STUMBLE is *stam* or *stem* (Pokorny 1021), providing STAMMER as a near cognate.

We don't seem to have the same misgivings about our upper extremities; hands and anything to do with hands

(IE *man*) yield strings of accomplished cognates with which we are entirely satisfied: MANAGE, COMMAND, MANDATE, MANUFACTURE and the like. We are even prouder of our flexible, opposable thumbs, often citing these as distinguished gifts elevating us biologically over our primate cousins. Thumbs up, we say. Still, revealing our innate habit of worry and nervousness, we say that a clumsy person is *all* thumbs.

4

NIGHTMARE, MURDER, AMBROSIA etc.

James Greenough and George Lyman Kittredge compiled a charming and exceedingly useful book on English etymology, titled *Words and Their Ways*, published first in 1900 and reprinted at intervals ever since. My paperback edition, dated 1962, is filled with information about the English language found in no other easily accessible source. I have only one problem with the book: the authors, eminences both, disapprove severely of the preoccupation with ancient roots which I find most entertaining and congenial, and openly disparage any effort to search for retained meanings inside the modern words built from such roots. It is nonsense, they say, to look for any meaning in a complex word beyond the immediate significance set by the context in which it is customarily used. The roots, especially those dating all the way back to Indo-European, are simply too old, and have been used in too many different ways, to have retained any vestige of their original sense.

They write,

> In the absolute sense of the term a word has no essential meaning. Words are conventional signs. They mean what they are intended to mean by the speaker and understood to mean by the hearer. . . . Something very different *was* the meaning a hundred or a thousand years ago, and between the two is a great gap, which the memory and the linguistic consciousness of the modern speaker does not span. . . . It is as if the word had been annihilated and created anew. The modern user knows nothing of the former meaning.

Perhaps so, but the earliest, antique *feeling* of certain roots persists, whether consciously perceived or not, inside some words, vibrating there alive, carrying the old significance into the depths of each new generation of cognates emerging in any language. Some words contain genetic markers.

Mer, for example, was the root for a nuclear family of descendant cousin words, almost all of which have retained at least traces of the family resemblance while being processed and reused in each of the major Indo-European languages. In some cases the relation is unmistakable, in others it is fainter, depending more on the light surrounding the word. The original significance of *mer*, calculated by the meaning of the earliest attested cognates, was to harm, to rub away, something foreboding real trouble. In early Germanic it became *maron*, a goblin; in Old English it was *mare*, and *maere*, an incubus sitting on the chest, smothering the victim; it was then incoporated in English NIGHTMARE, the dreaming and dreaming of death. In Sanskrit the root became *maranam*, death, dying. Greek took *mer* for part of *marainein*, to wither away, to lose flesh, and it moved into English as MARASMUS, a wasting disease. Latin provided an extended root to make *mordere* (with past participle *morsus*), meaning something which bites; English borrowed this for REMORSE and MORSEL, also MORBID. Words indicating aspects of dying and death appeared: *morthor* in Old English, MURDER in modern. Then MORTAL and MORTALITY, MORTMAIN (the dead hand of the law), MORTIFY and MURRAIN (a pestilence). MORT was the note on the huntsman's horn, sounded at the death of the deer. In Greek, the root was coupled with a negative, making *ambrotos*, the immortal divinities, and their potion AMBROSIA. Sanskrit had already done the same, (*a* plus *mrta*, death) to make *amrta*, IMMORTAL. Old Persian used *martiya*, a mortal man, to construct a word meaning man-eater, *martiyakhvara* (*khvara*, to eat) from which our mythological monster the MANTICORE evolved. The plain modern German word for pain, *smerd*, and our word SMART, are extensions of old *mer*. The same grim, attested meanings of death, dying, murder and mortality recur in words of Armenian, Lithuanian, Serbian, Baltoslavic, Old Church Slavonic, Avestan, Old Icelandic, and Old High German. The root *mer*, in short, has hung on intact through several millennia without losing its first intention as a word.

Mer seems to have only preserved, in a single cognate, the flat, literal message that it carried on its surface at the beginning: "to rub." This is to be found in our robust word MORTAR, the solid vessel used for grinding things up, with a pestle doing most of the work. (PESTLE, if you need to know, came from an IE root *peis*, with the meaning to crush, with cognates like PISTON and PILE, and from Greek *ptissein*, also meaning to crush or peel, the potable infusion *ptisan*, or TISANE. Also the PISTIL of a flower. Rather gentle cognates, carrying none of the enduring darkness of *mer*, and based more on the shape of the objects needed for the action.) In the case of *mer*, the inner essence was not an instrument, not any sort of object or shape, only the most ancient of ideas, the notion of slipping away from the earth.

Even MORTAR, in another usage, carries the old meaning of death. When needed, it became the lethal vessel, fat and open-mouthed, the source of mortar-fire, as much an immediate menace to the lives of infantry troops in this century's wars as anything yet devised by the arms industry.

It is a tribute to the stubbornness and conservatism of language that the *mer* played no role in the genesis of the collection of other important words containing the "mor" sound: MORES, MORAL, MORALS, MORALITY. These emerged from the root *me*, which simply meant one's state of mind. The MORES of a community are the customs, determined by how the members generally feel about each other; it is, generally, a good-humored, almost benign word. MORALE is pretty much the same feeling. MORALITY is what we've decided to agree on as a set of rules for living together, based on what we think of ourselves as people; it is rather nice to know that *moralis* was formed by Cicero to render the same meaning as Greek *ethicos*. Our ethics and morals, collectively, are rooted in our appraisal of humanity, and we are quite good about this, or anyway our hopes for this.

5

SNARE, NARCOTIC etc.

The root *sner* has a long record of enduring meaning, carrying the memory of a sort of darkness. The nineteenth-century philologists assigned it the ambiguous meaning to wind, to twist, and it has traveled through thousands of years bearing variations of such senses. It is an astonishment to have it now in modern English, in our word NARCOTIC. In between, it entered all sorts of words, sometimes with its meaning out on the surface, more often buried resonating inside, but always there. You could almost chart the posterity of *sner* with the diagrams of a family tree, or the sets of clades that evolutionary biologists design. One branch led to *snarkon* in Germanic and *snara* in Old Norse, a cord, trap or noose, and thence to our word SNARE. An offshoot on this line became Old English *nearu*, and modern English NARROW; Armenian made *nerger* to signify thin. A branch came into Greek as *narkoun* meaning numbness, and then, directly from this, *narcotik* in

27

Chaucer, and NARCOTIC in modern English, still with the sense of snaring but now something entrapping, addictive, combined with the separate sense of numbness. Chaucer wrote, *"He shall slepe as longue as ever the leste, the narkotykis and opijs ben so stronge."* In recent years the word has assumed a more general usage, applied to all sorts of illicit drugs, including cocaine.

So, the tracks of the root across time form a queerly logical series of transitions, from twisting and turning to the narrowness of a snare or noose, to more narrowness and thinness, emaciation, then dullness, numbness and stupefaction, and now today's street-vended plastic bags of heroin and crack.

But where, in all these cognates, is there a word to suggest anything like the rapture placed in the mind by NARCOTIC, or a sense of any high pleasure? Does *sner* have a secret offspring, carrying along a secret sense? It does, I think, but you must look at the word in the shadowed part of your mind. It was born very early in the language, in ancient Sanskrit, as *nrtyati*, he dances. Twisting, it turned into *nrtya*, then *nacca* in Prakrit, then *nac* in Hindi, and finally into an English word NAUTCH. A NAUTCH describes a northern Indian dance, performed slowly, twisting and winding, by a solitary girl dancer in shadow, accompanied by a solitary singer. Now you are inside the root, close to the dance in the mind.

Our word NARCOTIC has come a long, winding way from its old root, but it holds the oldest meaning alive inside. As it is used today, covering all classes of addictive drugs, it is no longer limited to the *numbness* sense;

there is nothing at all numbing about cocaine, much less a crack-smoker's high. Numbness won't do either for the feelings inserted into the brain by intravenous heroin. As for the latest addition to the marketplace, the smokable amphetamine derivative called *ice* (a nice example of the eloquence of street slang), this drug produces the very opposite of torpor; it unhinges the mind, explodes it, takes it and flings it wildly away from human discourse. It is twisting away from society itself.

6

DESIDERATUM, DESIRE etc.

Every now and then I have blundered into the word DE-
SIDERATUM, usually perched solidly, stolidly in the
middle of a too-long song of a sentence, blocking the
way, too many syllables to climb over; best just to move
around it hoping for smaller less gorgeous words, somehow prejudiced against any whole sentence containing
such an item. On the surface, from the very shape of it,
DESIDERATUM must mean something left to be desired,
something lacking but needed. The way I read it, DE-
SIDERATUM has its own desideratum. I can't recall ever
having heard it spoken aloud; if I have I must have let
it pass, one ear to the other.

Crankily, I looked it up last time I saw it, leafing
through an economist's essay on something. *Desire* is
obviously inside it, hiding in Latin, and my Latin dictionary says just that: something to be desired. "See
SIDEREAL," says Barnhart's *Etymology.* "See CON-
SIDER," says another.

Desideratum, Desire etc.

How can DESIRE, SIDEREAL and CONSIDER be cognates?

Well, consider the word. DESIRE has its own special feeling inside. It is not quite the same as wanting or wishing, not at all the sense of needing. When you desire something, or somebody, you're not about to get what you want; the object is not within reach or grasp, you need fortune to help you along. *Luck* is involved, always, or you would be using other words saying more plainly that you *have to have it,* and *will have it,* whatever. DESIRE is considerably made up of hope.

And so it says. The language started work on DESIRE long ago, and put it together meticulously. The beginning was the IE root *sweid* (also *sueid*), meaning simply to shine, anything glowing. It grew into *sweid-os,* then moved into Latin as *sidus,* a star, a constellation of stars. Reading the stars for portents, astrological assurances, produced the Latin term for augury, *considerare,* meaning to look at the stars carefully, to observe heaven for signs of luck. *Desiderare* came along naturally, as a close cognate but carrying much more urgency, a very strong wish for something special, but catchable only if the stars are right.

Thus our DESIRE, wanting it badly, even being tormented by the wanting, but always at risk of meeting the wrong pattern in the sky, the wrong stars. *Desiring* something is not just sitting around, hoping for it to drop in one's lap; the word implies effort, concentration, hard work, worry. Plus the layout in the sky. Plus fingers crossed.

So, it is a satisfaction to find in Pokorny that there

Et Cetera, Et Cetera

are actually two identical IE *sueid* roots. The philologists
have long assigned different meanings, separating the
two: the first *sueid* is our shining one, leading to old
desideratum and modern DESIRE; the second *sueid* produced *sudor* in Latin, *Schweiss* in German, SWEAT in
English. Glowing and perspiring, *shining* from the effort, the two roots are not all that far apart.

As an outsider, I hesitate to ask it, but perhaps the
etymologists might reconsider this small point. Only one
sueid root, connecting DESIRE and SWEAT as proper
cognates. I would like that.

7

SELF AND SOCIAL,
CONVERSATION etc.

The distinction between the notions of self and others must have been a subtle problem for the first makers of language, and the complexity is illustrated by the abundance and ambiguity of terms defining selfness and otherness in the IE family. The necessary lessons for the construction and endurance of a human community are embedded in the words used to elaborate the distinction. SELF (Old English *silf*) came from IE *seu*, also *swe*, (we our-)selves. From variants of these roots, we have a long list of words with *se-* as prefix, entities outside: SEPARATE SECEDE, SECLUDE, SECURE and the like. SURE is almost the same word as secure (*seure* in Middle English, from *securus* in Latin). *Solus* derives from *seu*, hence SOLO, SOLITUDE, SOLIPSISM and DESOLATE. *Swe* led to *suescere* in Latin, custom, and to *ethnos* in Greek. Starting with *ethnos* we have important words for what we are up to in society, what our crowd thinks and does: ETHICS, also ETHNIC. ETHICS is, in real life, an inclusive word for what we suppose ourselves to be, not just our crowd or our village; we have it in the language as a set of assumptions about the whole species, the ETHOS of humankind. The language thinks well of us, regardless of our customs, even when, as happens, we don't.

SOCIAL is the leading word, if you are casting about for a biological term for human beings, and the IE root for its origin is *sekw*, with the original meaning given as "to follow." I'm not so sure about the reading; *following* implies being led around these days, not moving in a group along a wilderness path, as it may have intended. One line of progeny led to Latin *socius* and thence to our SOCIABLE, SOCIETY and SOCIAL. Along the way, Sanskrit took *sakha* for friend and companion, Old English had *secq* with the same meanings, and, late on, English adopted SOCIAL as a particular word indicating friendliness and liking to live with others.

It is an etymological oddity that two other identical IE roots, both *sekw* (or *seku*), have been attested for what are considered quite different lines of words. One *sekw* is traced back to the meaning of perceive, and our word SEE came from this. The other meant to say, with our word SAY as a lineal descendant (also, curiously, the Old Norse word *skald*, a poet, and our word SCOLD, the noun, "a ribald or abusive person," often, occupationally, the same man).

It seems a coincidence beyond probability that three roots, all *sekw*, one with the clear meaning of social, could have entered language from unrelated sources. I prefer the notion, my unfounded own, that all three

*sekw*s came along from the Ur-language or languages
that must have existed before Indo-European, with companionship, friendship, seeing and saying all being connected parts of the necessary business of social living.

A CONVERSATION is the central, nearly defining activity of social living. It is easy enough to understand the
function of touching and odors in the social transactions
that underpin the social structure of an anthill, or a ter-
mitarium, or the complicated sounds and body movements (plus messages concerning polarized light and
lines of magnetic force) that regulate the households of
honeybees. For humans, small-talk is what we rely on.
Most of our conversations are exchanges of signals dem-
onstrating the reality and closeness of the participants,
holding them in companionship. We depend heavily on
small-talk for our cohesion; the weather, the time of
day, the turn of seasons, the current births and deaths,
topics used not so much for any intrinsic interest as for
just holding us together. Most of what appears all day,
all night on our television screens is, essentially, small-
talk.

From time to time, conversations turn to matters of
significance, and large social decisions emerge. The
older meaning of CONVERSATION is of interest here. The
word came from the IE root *wer*, meaning to turn, to
move around a place, to frequent a neighborhood. Doing
these things together was the origin of our word, not
talking, certainly nothing like small-talk. CONVERSA-
TION was the word for the behavior of people, their
manner of life together. Later the meaning expanded to
indicate one's associates, a circle of acquaintances. Only

recently did talking take over the word, although the earlier meanings still resound inside. A *conversation piece* is not really an item of furniture or an eccentric piece of sculpture displayed to stir up talking; it was a genre of painting depicting groups of human beings simply being *social*, one way or another, maybe talking, maybe not. These paintings were enormously popular in their time, but the fashion faded away. The people in the paintings were, as it turned out, *too* fashionable, and the word SOCIETY had begun to assume one of its current distortions — as we used to say, "high society."

I wish we could have CONVERSATION back with its early meaning. One of the nicest things about us is our pleasure in simply being *together*, talking to each other about one thing or another but not necessarily talking at all, just there in an amiable arrangement, a *conversation*. When such a gathering of us is really working at its very best, with affection all round, the long silences turn out to be the nicest moments for memory. It goes without saying, as the saying goes.

8

——

SMALL-TALK, SLEEP,
DREAM etc.

Speaking of small-talk, it is surprising how much of the time and energy of language is invested in the more or less mechanical exchange of words. If you were to count up the words, and the breaths drawn, something over ninety percent of the remarks made in a day's turning are essentially idle sounds, many of them intended only as reminders to others that a potential speaker of language is at hand if needed. A great part of what is called conversation is simply the transmission of sounds indicating presence, politeness, interest if interest is wanted, readiness to talk.

It is another surprise that the activity that consumes a full third of our total lifespan, *sleeping*, even more of our time in infancy (*that* word, by the way, *in* plus *fans*, simply means unable to speak, which may be the reason babies — (and cats) — sleep so much) goes almost unacknowledged in the roots of language. One root indicating sleep is *drem*, from which we have French *dormir*

Et Cetera, Et Cetera

and our DORMANT and DORMITORY, not particularly descriptive, not even allusive. Another root, *sleb*, signified both weakness and sleep, while still another, *leb*, meaning to hang loosely or LAPSE, COLLAPSE, has been claimed by some authorities. It is a curiosity of language that both *leb* and *sleb* have been mentioned in dictionaries as candidate roots for the word LABOR, perhaps because of the connection to weakness, exhaustion, slipping, collapsing, even sleeping, but the philologists do not ELABORATE on this.

DREAMING, the chief preoccupation of that thirty-three percent of our lives, is strangely overlooked as well. The language has *drem* for sleep, of course, but despite the similarity of sound there are no successor words meaning dream, or anything like it. There is *dhreugh*, with a Germanic suffixed form *draugma* leading to Old English *dream*, but this word was used to describe music and joy and wonderful visions, and had nothing to do with sleeping, and there is no direct evidence for the meaning we attach to DREAM today. It could be that the language, in a sleepy moment, got *drem* and *dhreugh* mixed up together, with sleep and joy and music all combined. If so, the language has had better dreams than most of the rest of us.

Actually, *dhreugh* had quite another intention. In its original form it meant illusion, delusion, and as it developed in some of the languages it took on the meaning of outright deception. The Avestan cognate was *druzaiti*, he lies, he deceives, while Sanskrit *druhyati* took it further, he damages, he hurts.

I suppose the case can be made that dreams are really

lies, or as the analysts prefer, truth turned upside down, and this is the message of *dhreugh*. After all, there should be plenty of other words for deception, not decorated by the ideas of joy and music surrounding Old English *dream*. But the truth is, there are not many such words with Indo-European ancestors, suggesting that either the roots were lost, laid aside and forgotten, or Indo-European was a more truthful language than ours. The only IE root I can find in my dictionaries for flat-out lying is *leugh*, meaning just that. The root grew into Germanic as *liogan* (modern German has *lugen*), Old English *leogan* and *ligan;* in Old Slavic to lie was *lugati*, in Lithuanian *lugoti*, in English LIE, BELIE and, of all things, WARLOCK (originally a literal oath-breaker, Old English *waerloga*).

Our other words for lying seem to be inventions of later languages, some of them sounding evasive in their own construction. *Mend* is an IE root meaning a physical defect, a fault; it appeared in Latin as *mendicus*, a beggar, and *mendax*, a liar, and we have it as MENDACIOUS. The Latin *falsus* had alternative meanings of false, a lie, or simply mistaken, misled, wrong. Some have suggested the IE root *ghwel*, meaning crooked, for FALSE, connecting it to Greek *phelos*, deceitful, Sanskrit *hvalati*, he goes astray, and Lithuanian *zvalus*, clever, but there is disagreement on the matter; false may turn out to be a rootless word. Deceive is a contraption of a word, with *kap* as the IE root, meaning grasp, leading to the Latin *capere*, to take, thence to *decipere* (*de*, away, plus *capere*, to take), the whole thing, DECEIVE, meaning (somehow) "to catch in a trap." The Latin

Et Cetera, Et Cetera

fraudo meant to cheat, embezzle, hence FRAUD, but no known earlier root. BETRAYAL came from IE *do*, to give, Latin *tradere*, and is assigned the derivation "to give over." It seems as though the language has to work hard contriving more and more complicated metaphors for lying: dissembling, prevarication, dreaming and the like. One gathers that it dislikes the whole idea.

Truth, on the other hand, abounds in roots and cognates, streaming through the language. *Deru*, of course, the TREE, something solid, TRUTH, TRUST. *Per* for PROBITY. *Kand*, to shine, for CANDOR. *Sem*, one, *ker*, to grow, *sem-kers*, "of one growth": SINCERE. *Kerd*, heart, and *dhe*, place, for CREDENCE. *Reg*, right, for RECTITUDE, CORRECT. *Wero*, true, for VERITY, VERACIOUS. Truth to tell, I do like the looks of this set of metaphors, much more than the claptrap collection of evasive mistakes and misreadings of the facts, clumsy constructs all, a veritable tissue of lies.

9

TELL, RECKON, ERR etc.

An ordinary, everyday word for using language is to TELL, from IE *del*, which had the meaning tell as well as numerous cognates with the same meaning and sound. We have TALE and TALK from *del*, by way of Old English *talu*, Middle Dutch and Old Icelandic *tala*, speech. But as *del* passed through other Germanic languages it took on added responsibilities: in Old High German *zala* became number, (*Zahl* in modern German); in Gothic *talzan* meant to teach. Our bank TELLER turned up in Middle English around 1475, keeping accounts. Oddly, ancient Greek took *del* for a very telling word *dolos*, craftiness; Latin made *dolus*, guile, deceit.

Something similar to the turn of *del* to tell, tale, talk and calculating happened in the evolution of our words ACCOUNT and COUNT. An account is in one sense a tale, a narrative; so is the recounting of a story. Both derive from count, which is in its first sense a numbering of items in a set, a reckoning. To count is also an affirmation: I count myself lucky. All the words have the same IE root, *peu*, to stamp or cut something. Latin took *peu* for *putare*, to prune, clean, consider, which we have in English PUTATIVE, supposed, presumed. On another line, Latin produced *computare*, to calculate, compute together, and this became Old French *cunter*, *conter*, and Old English *count*, a reckoning. The words AC-COUNT and RECOUNT, with their meaning of narrating tales, seem to have carried this sense simultaneously, which is a strange, small feat of language.

RECKON is a word carrying the meanings of thinking about, considering, looking at all sides, and counting up, computing. It comes from a grand IE root *reg*, in the company of a long list of dignitary cognates. *Reg* originally had the sense of moving in a straight line, leading, ruling. Suffixed as *reg-to*, it came into Germanic as *rehtaz* and Old English as *riht*, meaning RIGHT, correct, straight, just. In Latin it became *regere*, to lead, guide, from which we have such words as RECTITUDE and CORRECT. Back in Germanic the root turned to *rakinaz*, ready, straightforward, and *rikenin*, to count up, answer for, consider. Middle English had *reckining* with the sense of a narrative report, as in account and recount, before 1325. The modern word RECKON has thus been in the language, in one sense or the other, for a very long time, but always with its modern meaning of calculating, computing. But when we actually use the word, saying I reckon such-and-such, we are guessing, as always.

RECK, meaning to take heed, be concerned, and RECKLESS are cognates from the same family. Germanic had *rokjan,* meaning careful, paying attention, and Old English took *rokja* to make *receleas,* careless, RECK-LESS. Both come from *reg,* of course, a small textbook on how to get on in human affairs.

Another root, *ers,* meaning to be in motion, comes at the same problem from the opposite direction. An Old Germanic cognate, *res, ras* in Old Norse, signified rushing headlong, and is the source of English RACE. The lesson is contained in the other cognates, beginning with an extension of the IE root *ersa,* taken up by Latin as *errare,* which meant to wander, stray, rove about. The ultimate destination of such a word becomes clear in the stream of new words on their way toward modern English. Old English had *ierre,* with the combined meaning of anger and straying off, impatience, frustration, maybe influenced by the similar Latin *ira,* anger, from which we have IRE and IRATE. Old Saxon had *irri,* angry, and *irron,* astray. Gothic had *airzeis,* meaning led astray, misled.

Wandering about, being misled, misinformed, is a source of anger, clear enough. But look at the language's management of the later words. Old French continued the wandering sense, in *errer* and *errant,* and Chaucer used *erraunt* in *Canterbury Tales* for traveling, roving. Chaucer also used *erratik* in *Troilus and Cressida,* borrowed from Old French *erratique,* with much the present sense of unpredictability and mistaken moves, ERRATIC. Finally, the root comes to full maturity with all its significance, wandering and wondering in our words ERR and ERROR. It is the way we are, not in any sense an ABERRATION.

10

RUMOR, IRONY, ARGUMENT etc.

The language keeps talking about itself, cannot seem to have enough of itself. At a guess, I'd say there are more roots for the various ways of using language than for all other human activities together, some of them hidden away inside longer words that seem to be designed for other purposes, most of them standing baldly out in full view. The language, in fact, spends a large part of the time calling attention to what it can accomplish.

Some words keep their heads down, fingers in ears, waiting behind the tree for their impact, hoping always for the worst. RUMOR is an example. On the surface it seems a quiet word, almost a whisper, one low voice to a cupped ear. But it has a necessary magnitude; the word rumor is never used for something you heard yesterday afternoon in a bar, unless that something is itself a rumor, a rumor of a rumor in effect. If you heard so-and-so say that stock will go up in three days, that is not a rumor. But if so-and-so says, "I've been hearing that that stock is going up," it begins to qualify as a rumor, and later, if you hear ten other people say something like that, in different bars at different times, *now* you have a rumor. It is not at all a quiet word, it is a bomb of a word, requiring the collective energy of many minds and voices to bring it into existence.

The language knows this, and it put the word RUMOR together with care for its meaning, having selected its parentage thoughtfully. The IE root is *reu*, with the original sense of bellow, nothing less. In Old Norse, *reu* became *rauta*, to roar; from *rauta* we have English ROUT. Taken into Latin, *reu* produced *rugire*, ROUT, RUT; Latin *raucus* was a hoarse shout, RAUCOUS. Latin *rumor* itself was a widespread noise, a clamor, an explosion. Greek *oryesthai* was a howl, a great outcry, Sanskrit *ravati* was a loud shout. Over time, and with the sort of reflection that only the language itself can devote to a single word, English took RUMOR for the meaning it has today: something *about* to explode, something not yet quite ready but, just ahead, a roaring shout, a scandal.

Sometimes the roots for speaking are still in view, but the real meaning of the word depends on slight modifications made so long ago as to be forgotten. *Wer* was an IE root meaning simply to speak, entering Greek as *eirein*, to say. With a slight twist, *eirein* was turned into *eiron*, one who says less than he thinks, a dissembler, and then into *eironeia*, feigned ignorance, with its Socratic (and present) meaning of using words to convey the opposite of their literal significance. Latin picked it up as *ironia*, IRONY, and it was adopted thus by English in the sixteenth century.

To argue is, of course, to make something or other perfectly clear to someone, and no wonder that the root is *arg*, meaning shining or white. It places argue and argument alongside *argyrol*, an antiseptic silver (*argentine*) salt once used for painting infected tonsils, also *arginine*, an amino acid unrelated to silver but with white crystals. But if you try to take *arg* farther there is trouble. An *argosy* is a large merchant ship, not necessarily shining, white or silver, named by Greeks from the Adriatic port Ragusa. *Argon*, a colorless inert gas, gets its name because of inertness, *a* plus *ergon*, without work. *Argot*, street talk, comes from French and has no known origin. An *argus* pheasant has a tail with brilliantly colored shapes resembling eyes, and is named for the mythical many-eyed giant Argus, no connection to *arg*. But ARGIL is a useful white clay, prized by potters, and is based on *arg*. You need guides before setting your mind on IE roots.

The plainest, most unambiguous word for speaking the language is SPEAK, from IE *spreg*, which meant, plainly, to speak. The word came into Germanic steadily enough, but occasionally exploded like speech as it came along. The sense of speak was unaltered in Old High German *spehhan*, Middle Dutch *speken*, Old Saxon *sprecan* and Old English *sprecan*, but in Old Icelandic *spraka* meant to rattle, and *spraki* was a report, a rumor. Swedish has *spraka* as crackle, sparkle. Sanskrit *sphurjati* is to burst forth, to crackle and rattle, so is Lithuanian *sprageti*. The Welsh cognate is *ffreg*, to chatter, gossip. And the Greek *spharageisthai* is to crackle or hiss. SPEAKING is itself a word almost always on the very edge of going out of control, or so it seems.

11

——

LOGOS etc.

The most puzzling, ambiguous and mysterious of all words for words is the earliest, the original Word in the beginning, *Logos*. When John wrote his tremendous Greek sentence: *In the beginning was the Word,* he used *Logos* in a larger sense than any word in itself, or any set of words. He intended, I take it, even more than the Word as speech. *Logos* combined the meaning of reason, thought, discourse, all the events in the human mind that are set in action by language, the source of world order and comprehensibility. In the Gospel of John, *Logos* was the thought and wish of God, a member of the Trinity. The word was holy.

Logos had a humble beginning. The IE root was *leg,* meaning collect, with derivatives meaning generally to speak. *Leg* became *log-o* and Greek *logos,* signifying variously reason, speech, word, and from this word we have LOGIC, LOGISTIC, and strings of words prefixed by LOGO- or suffixed by -LOGUE and -LOGY (etymol-

——

ogy for instance). Some of the other *leg* cognates are fascinating, and puzzling. Germanic *lekjas* was a speaker of magic words, an enchanter, moving into Old English as *laece*, then LEECH, the old term for the doctor (also, ambiguously, the blood-sucking worm employed by the doctor). Latin *legere*, meaning to gather, collect, pick up and read, produced our words LECTURE, LEGEND, LESSON, COLLECT, INTELLIGENT and SELECT, plus LEGIBLE. The Greek *legein*, to gather, speak, provided DIALOGUE, LEXICON, CATALOGUE, LOGARITHM. Latin made *leg* into *lex*, the law, from which we have LEGAL, LEGISLATE, LEGITIMATE, PRIVILEGE and LOYAL; *leg* also became *legare* in Latin, thus our LEGACY, LEGATE, ALLEGE, COLLEAGUE, DELEGATE.

Left far behind, essentially out of mind, almost soundless within *Logos*, was its original meaning of language, human speech, the faculty making everything else possible for humanity, including complete theological systems. And there, almost at the horizon, remains the first IE root, *leg*, still collecting words streaming out like a comet's tail behind *Logos*, the beginning.

12

——

BITE to BOAT, SALT to SALARY, SWEET to SUAVE etc.

Often enough, the lists of words derived from the same root seem to make no sense when lined up in a row, but looked at closely they do, almost always. *Bheid*, for example, is a root for which the original meaning was to split, with Germanic derivatives referring to biting. Our word BOAT is tracked by the scholars to *bheid*. How come?

BITE itself makes perfectly good sense, of course, also BEETLE, both turning up in Germanic and Old English as *bitan*. A BIT fits nicely, something BITTEN off, also BITTER, from the biting taste; also BAIT, considering hunting hounds, tethered prey, all that.

But what about BOAT? Easy, as it turns out. The earliest watercraft were dugout contraptions, canoes, coracles, their insides dug out, not bitten literally, but surely something like.

How did we connect SALT and SALARY; why say that someone is worth his SALT? The IE root is *sal*, taken into Latin as *salarium,* "money given to soldiers to buy salt, hence any allowance, pay." A SOLDIER contains the same idea, incidentally; the word comes from *solidus,* the coin used for pay. SOUSE came along as the word for salted meat, later anything pickled, still later anybody the same. The Greek *als* was a lump of salt, also the sea; *alsis* was something leaping. Our word SALTATION (leaping, dancing) has been assigned a different root, *sel,* but the notions of jumping and salt are still mixed together; Latin has *salire,* to leap, to jump around, also *saliens,* sacrificial salt "which, as a good omen, leapt up when thrown into the fire." Frogs and toads belong to the order SALENTIA.

And there is SWEET, from the IE *swad,* which had the meaning sweet, also pleasant. Nicely, *swad* has provided us with SUASION, PERSUASION, SWEET-TALK. Also, sweetly, SUAVE, from the Latin *suavis,* delightful. Greek moved swades to *hedos,* pleasure, from which we have HEDONISM.

But then Greek gave it a negative twist: *A-edes,* not pleasant, disagreeable. Later, New Latin picked up the word, and we have it as AEDES, any old mosquito.

13

FASTIDIOUS, ANSWER, GRAMMAR etc.

FASTIDIOUS has been in the English language since at least as far back as the fourteenth century. Today its dictionary definition is "careful in every detail, difficult to please, meticulous." As recently as 1755, Samuel Johnson's dictionary gives *fastidious* the meaning of "disdainful, delicate to a vice, insolently nice." Parenthetically, he lists NICE with several meanings, none of them particularly nice, one of them simply "fastidious, squeamish." Another Johnson definition of *nice* is "often used to express a culpable delicacy." In the original sense, from the Latin *fastidium*, FASTIDIOUS carried an almost violent meaning of revulsion and aversion, a disgust that has left only traces in the word. Today, to be fastidious suggests somebody delicate, rather fragile, fussy. The IE root *bhar* forecast both early and late meanings. *Bhar*, a bristle, a bur, became *fastus* in Latin, meaning prickly, something like current slang for the personality of a fastidious man or woman.

Fastidious, Answer, Grammar etc.

How do changes like this occur in the language, and who is responsible? METICULOUS has had a similar transformation, shifting from its early meaning of fearful (because of the Latin root *metus*, fear), to today's fastidious care for the fine details of an action.

Scholars are not the changers of word meanings, nor are governments or their agencies, not even the Immortals of the French Academy (although protection of the language is their sole statutory obligation.) Nobody seems to have the power to control or even slow down the shifting senses of words, not even the French.

When a word like NICE can exist unchanged in its structure and sound for a thousand years or longer, and during that time move from the meaning of an ignorant, silly person (*ne* plus *scire*, not-knowing) all the way to today's sense of decency in a person (a nice man), or exact precision in a thought (a nice distinction), would seem to demand a process of deliberation and open discussion. But it is not so, as far as we know. The word simply changed. Something like this happened to SILLY, but in reverse. Early on, a silly person was a happy one; the IE root was *sel*, meaning happy; cognates are HILARIOUS and EXHILARATE. The early SILLY was not just happy, it also carried an air of innocence. But now, and for the past several centuries, a silly man is simply foolish, trivial, lacking sense, even stupid. Who decided that?

It is a silly question and a nice question, in both early and late meanings, a foolish question and a happy sharp question today. Long ago some unknown influence was installed in language to enable it to change itself. It is,

Et Cetera, Et Cetera

I think, an extremely happy thought that language is a live thing, a creature off on its own, capable of making its own transformations in meaning whenever it has a mind to. No attempts to meddle or intervene on the part of the participants, you and I, can have the slightest effect, any more than a single termite can affect the decisions of the Hill and its million residents. It gives me the same relaxed satisfaction as my conviction that I have no real governance over the workings of my own brain, nor am I obliged to run my liver or keep track of my bone marrow. For all the overarching importance of language in our lives, it is nice to know that we don't have to worry about it; it will look after itself, change itself, expand its power, all on its own.

The IE root *dhabh* had the general meaning of fitting together; its Germanic cognates indicated fitting behavior, gentleness, mildness; in Old English it became *gedaefte*, later *dafte*, a nice person to have around. Gradually, the language decided otherwise, and DAFT is now crazy, mad, obsessed in English speech; the Scots have held out longer for the old sense, using DAFT for frolicsome, someone only slightly touched.

Ask a silly question, you get a silly answer. Even these plain old words have been altered, or have altered themselves. Before 1200, a QUESTION was a *question*, a philosophical or theological problem, nothing more or less. The Latin *quaestionem*, and Old French *question*, referred to a legal investigation. An ANSWER was an *andswere* in Middle English, *andswaru* in Old English, two words, anti and swear. It is good to know that the same process occurred in Sanskrit, using quite different

Fastidious, Answer, Grammar etc.

words. Sanskrit's answer is *prativacanum: prati,* against, plus *vacanum,* to speak. Today, an answer is simply a RESPONSE, but have a careful look at that *response, re,* back, plus *spondere,* to promise; it carries its own version of *answer* inside, a heavier commitment than most of us think we are taking on when we respond. The IE root is *spend,* meaning to make an offering, perform a ritual act, vow, with cognates SPOUSE and SPONSOR. There is no easy answer, if you keep looking over your shoulder.

Here is another quiet change. Today's word for eating dinner, to DINE, comes to us from a Latin word meaning to fast. The Latin was *jejunus,* empty, hungry, from which we have our word *jejune,* a dull, empty person, and *jejunum,* the flat, usually empty portion of the small intestine. The beginning of DINE and DINNER was *disjejunare,* to break one's fast, becoming *disjunare* then *disner* in Old French, finally our triumphant words DINE and DINNER.

The grammar we use today has changed to some extent, but not fundamentally. Rules governing word order in modern English are rather different from the regulations in Old English and the other more Germanic languages. We have freed our speech of the tangle of inflections that used to beset it, and our grammar provides English with a flexibility perhaps matched only by Chinese. But the word GRAMMAR is itself almost a brand-new word, meaning something much more technical and specialized than it did originally. At the beginning, when *grammar* moved as *gramere* into Middle

English from the Old French *gramaire* and Latin *grammatica*, it signified the art of writing, especially the making of letters in constructing written words. The IE root was *gerebh*, meaning to scratch or carve. The art was a subject of mystery, the grammarians were believed to be magicians. The image of grammar as a form of magic persisted for some centuries; indeed the word came into Scottish as *glamourie*, and a sense of magic still lurks within the modern word GLAMOUR.

We are still at it, inventing new words and watching them being incorporated into the language or being rejected out of hand, depending on how the language feels about them. Sometimes mistakes are made, even errors that ought to be embarrassments, but once the language makes up its mind the words persist. A rather sweet example of getting things wrong is the modern technical term for a marvelous species of lemur, living in Madagascar, named by the formal nomenclature of mammalogists *Indri indri*. The naming was done by the early-nineteenth-century French naturalist Pierre Sonnerat, who saw the animal while exploring in a forest and heard one of his native guides exclaim in excitement, "Indri! Indri!" Much later it was realized that *indri*, in Madagascar language, meant "Look! Look at that!" but by that time the word was already in the dictionaries, perhaps leaving the philologists to be puzzled by the resemblances to the Sanskrit word *Indriyati*, meaning to perceive or sense things in the world, and raising a new scholarly question: How did Sanskrit ever get to Madagascar?

14

ETYMON, YES, SIN etc.

ETYMON has no etymon, fittingly enough. It existed only in Greek, with the generally accepted meaning of a true word, the original word, the source of all related words to come later. But it is hard to be sure about this. How could a word like ETYMON appear out of nowhere and suddenly install itself in ancient Greek, out of the blue, so to say. It is also strange that there seem to be no descendant words based on ETYMON, apart from the obvious immediate derivatives: ETYMOLOGY, ETYMOLOGIST, ETYMOLOGIZE. All this would make ETYMON unique, unprecedented. The OED suggests a possible way to bypass the puzzle. The philologist Brugmann, a century ago, proposed an origin for *etymon* in Old Aryan, *s-etumos*, with the suffixed *s* derived from IE *es*, meaning it is, it is true. If this were correct, it would not only provide *etymon* with proper ancestors but would also assure a huge number of cousins.

Es is one of the most prolific of all IE roots in the

language. At the outset, it had the meaning to be, extending as *es-mi* in Germanic and *eam* in Old English
to modern AM; and from *es-ti* to German *ist* to French
est to English IS. It turned up again in Old English *sie*,
meaning it is so, *si* in romance languages, and our word
YES. And again it moved as *sont* to *soth* in Old English,
and to SOOTH (forsooth) and SOOTHE.

The connection of SOOTHE to YES is strange but
true; it takes a bit of relaxing to get it straight in the
mind. I suppose that if something *is*, and is true, and
leads to nodding of the head, and brings the archaic
response *sooth*, or the modern answer *yes*, it is a soothing experience. The truth is not always soothing, but in
a better world it ought to be.

There is more. Somehow, the notion of truth, in an
imperfect world, needs a word for telling the truth about
us even when we are not at our best. *Es* was used for
this, shifting to *sundjo* in Germanic, to *synn* in Old English, to *sinne* in Middle English, to SIN, to be wrong,
to do wrong, to have the truth told, even the truth about
ourselves.

Es became *esse* in Latin, to be, and yielded a burst
of words: ESSENCE, ENTITY, PRESENT and QUINTES-
SENCE, the fifth and highest essence, after earth, air, fire
and water. Latin produced *prodesse*, to be beneficial,
today's PROUD.

Greek took *es* to make *einai*, to be, and constructed
the roots for our ONTOLOGY, the study of being, and ON-
TOGENY, the becoming and development of living things.
Also BIONT, one of the useful words for a living organism.

Sanskrit had *satya* for truth and reality, and SATYA-

GRAHA was the term for Mahatma Gandhi's nonviolent resistance against the British occupiers.

Underlying almost all the families of words derived from *es* is the notion of truth. YES says this: yes, it is true. It is a rather nice surprise to find this idea so threaded through what has become our quite ordinary day-to-day discourse. Some of our other words for true, unrelated to this one, are almost as ubiquitous and just as surprising. The IE root for the very word true is *deru*, originally meaning something solid and enduring. It became TRUE by way of Germanic *dreu*, and also turned into *traust* in Old Norse, from which we have TRUST. By another route, in the Latin *durare*, we have ENDURE. Early on, *deru* formed TREE, and came into Gaelic as DRUID (*deru* plus *wid*, to know), a priestly elder who knew the truth about trees.

It is redundant to say that something is *very* true, also probably poor grammar, but I do like the resonance of the two words together. The very word VERY has the literal meaning of true, thanks to its Latin parent *verus*, true, and its IE root *weros*, and its cousins VERACITY, VERITY, VERIFY and AVER. VERY TRUE has a nice sound, after all. The scholars argue over the inclusion of SEVERE on the list, because of uncertainty about how to find an appropriate meaning in the *se* or *sed* prefix. Still, there it stands in Latin, *severitas*, meaning gravity, sternness, even harshness, qualities not infrequently associated with the truth, especially the truth about oneself. Not to mention difficulties of the same sort with PERSEVERE, although this word does mean, among other things, looking for truth.

15

———

GORGEOUS, GARGOYLE,
SURLY etc.

There are some words we simply won't have around the house, not because of their nastiness — although some of them qualify for that word (questionably derived from an even nastier-sounding root *nizdo*, a bird's NEST, by way of Old French *nastre*, something strange and bad, Middle English *nasti*, NASTY, not a good word for the birds' nests in our tree), but because they don't mean at all what they are trying to say, and contain mendacious roots.

GORGEOUS is high on our list of such words, never used. Instead of signifying any sort of splendor or magnificence, and despite the dictionary meanings of "wonderful, delightful," there is an undertow of tawdriness in this word. Its base is another word, GORGE, coming from the IE root *gwere*, meaning to swallow, yielding GARGLE, CRAG, GARGOYLE, CRAW, words like that, not remotely gorgeous. One etymological guess is that people have been wearing ornaments around their throats

Gorgeous, Gargoyle, Surly etc.

forever, gorgets, necklaces, baubles, and some of these may have seemed impressive enough to call for commendation. But GORGEOUS is the wrong word, with a wrong root, and bad cognates all around. In another off moment, the language might well have given us *jugularious* for the same purpose. GORGEOUS is a cheap word, like the imitations of the lace worn by Saint Audrey* of Ely to hide her goiter (that word coincidentally has the same root, *gwere*).

PORTLY is another, and PORTENTOUS might as well be taken off as well. PORTLY was once used to suggest a stately and majestic bearing, but it also implies just comfortably fat, and I don't see why anyone should easily or necessarily be both in the same word, although I can understand the hopes of the corpulent, middle-aged Middle Englishmen who invented it. Literally, PORTLY must have been *port-like,* with port carrying its meaning of *carriage, bearing, mien.* The very word PORTLY strikes me as a kind of pretention. Wallace Stevens had it right, in *Anecdote of a Jar:* "I placed a jar in Tennessee . . . the jar was round upon the ground, and tall and of a *port* in air. . . . It did not give of bird or bush."

PORTENTOUS ought to mean *portending,* foretelling the future, presaging, with a kernal of danger and warning inside. But it has been set upon in the language,

---

* St. Audrey lace became *'taudrey lace,* neckties sold at fairs in her honor after her death in A.D. 679. A similar change occurred in the name of Saint Anthony, the patron saint of swineherds: small pigs were first called by his name, later *tantonies;* still later tantony became a term for a person who follows another obsequiously (OED).

turned into a word with all the magical magisterial fore-casting gone, leaving only the prodigious, vaguely pre-posterous image.

There are certain words that seem overweight, just looking at them on a page, even hearing them sounded. OBESE is itself a fat word, fatter when inspected closely: Latin *ob*, away, plus *edere*, eat (IE *ed*), eating away without even glancing up. OTIOSE also has a fat look; it pretends to mean at leisure but is really lazy, doing nothing, capable of nothing until reversed by the prefix *ne*, then becoming NEGOTIATE and getting down to business.

Perhaps I have an unconscious prejudice against words beginning with *o*, particularly capital *O*, and most of all most words with the prefix *ob*. I dislike OBITUARY, for instance, not out of any distaste for the subject but because of the parsimony of the roots inside the word. *Ob*, down, plus *ire* to go, Latin *obire*, to die. Past participle *obitus*, hence the news item. Sometimes the language doesn't seem to have its mind on its work, slacking off, trying to ride on its reputation, otiose. Some words simply won't do.

Some other *o*'s: OBNOXIOUS, OBLOQUY, OBSE-QUIOUS, OBSESS. Just look at OBSESS. *Ob*, this time meaning on or against, plus *sed*, to sit, beset, Latin *obsessus*, all of it meaning something like sitting on, sitting against, being sat on. A word intended for the strength of OBSESS has nothing inside to back it up. It is language with its mind on something else, maybe obsessed by something else. It won't do.

Gorgeous, Gargoyle, Surly etc.

OFFAL, a perfectly awful word, nothing to hold it in place except the meagre root *apo:* off, away. No conceivably related word among its cognates except maybe DEPOSIT. The language on an otiose weekend. OMINOUS.

The earth is an "OBLATE solid," it says, meaning a stretched sphere, fatter at its middle than the distance between its poles, *spheroidal,* it says, unattractively. I don't like the word OBLATE, especially when applied to the earth with the sense, as I read it, of imperfection. The geometric fault is not improved by the compromise term *spheroidal,* because of that odious suffix *-oid.* I cannot put up with anything *-oid,* if you want to know. Homin*oid,* for example; if the language is in doubt about it, it ought to come down on one side or the other, either subhuman primate or human, don't waffle around with any "*oids*"; *hominid* is no better, a weasel word. It doesn't sound nice. And if left as it is, with today's systematists as obsessively reductionist about paleoanthropological osteology as they are professionally obliged to be, and with all the new old bones from African landslides and caves, we will soon be reading *humanoidoid,* an onomastic oxymoron, adding insult to injury.

OLEAGINOUS is an ONEROUS, OOZING word.

And I don't much like the turn of language that inserted OGLE into speech. I can't stand the sight of the word, much less its oily sound. I don't need reminding that it came from the root *okw,* EYE, and I'd as soon forget the Germanic derivative *oog.*

I have never encountered a sentence beginning with

O, or *Oh!* that I gladly went on to read, not in verse, not in prose. When I catch sight of such a line, I think: Oh well; something ominous is on its way.

This has turned itself into a surly essay, and that's a note to end on. SURLY is itself the surliest word on my list. I would wish it out of existence if I could. But it is redeemed, in part, by its usefulness as a piece of social history. Skeat lists it as derived from Old English *sur-lic*, sour-like, from Germanic *sauer*, and it feels like that. But others, including the OED, tell a much more interesting story, tracing it to Middle English *sirly*, formed from *sir* and *like*. At its outset, it carried somewhat the meaning of lordly, noble, imperious, although the IE root was simply *sen*, meaning old, SENIOR; the Irish SHANTY, an old shack, comes from the same root. Gradually, the language took possession of the word, giving it more the feeling that language users-at-large tend to have in regard to the class of men officially labeled as upper in station and power. The spelling change is first noted in 1566, in a translation of Horace's *Satires*, and perhaps the change to SURLY was influenced by CHURL, applied in the fifteenth century to freemen of the lowest rank in Britain. SURLY plummeted from its noble station, and took on the meaning of CHURLISH. Both shared in common the sense of bad manners, rudeness and the moroseness that one properly associates with this cast of mind.

16

F - - - etc.

Here comes the most commonly used and shocking taboo word in the English language. Fifty years ago it
could not have been placed in a printed book without
strong objections from editors and publishers, let alone
readers. Even today, although it was listed in several
editions of the American Heritage Dictionary during the
early 1970s with a scholarly note on its likely origins,
someone thought better and removed it from all editions
of that dictionary after 1983. Whenever newspapers feel
obliged to allude to the word, in verbatim news accounts, the convention is to print f - - -. The word, of
course, is FUCK. The very sight of the whole word, there
on a page, is still a shock. Not at all because of the
sexual meaning, which by this time, in an age of open
frankness about all sexual matters, has almost been lost.
The word shocks because of the explosive violence contained in it, the malevolence, the expression of contempt.

Et Cetera, Et Cetera

Its first meaning remains, of course, sexual intercourse, but the several other, meaner meanings are: "to deal with in an aggressive, unjust or spiteful manner. ... to mishandle; bungle . . . , usually used with *up*, to meddle or interfere."* If you are strolling past a construction site in mid-Manhattan, you will surely hear this word used more frequently than any other in the English language, and you are just as likely to hear it repeatedly around the computer consoles in pleasant Wall Street offices on a bad business day.

The word's original root and its cognates in other tongues are matters of etymological dispute. Watkins† assigned *peig* (or *peik*) as the IE root, with the meaning of "evil-minded, hostile," although this reference vanishes in the 1985 edition.‡ The English-German dictionary published by Langenscheidt in 1984 lists *ficken* as the German equivalent (accompanied by a symbol indicating *unanstandig*, indecent). Pokorny provides an Old Icelandic word derived from *peig*, *feikn*, meaning ruined, spoiled, a modern German word *feige*, cowardly, several other terms in Old Germanic and Sanskrit signifying doom and death in general, but no *ficken* that I can find. And the English word seems totally orphaned.

The Oxford English Dictionary has never listed it among the numberless words in the standard editions, but now it has appeared in the Supplement Volume I, citing the item as a taboo word. But surely not taboo because of the sexual meaning. On other pages of the

*American Heritage Dictionary, 1969–1973 editions.
†AHD, 1973
‡AHD, 1985.

F - - - etc.

standard OED one can find any numb
sexually explicit, certainly more des⟨
has been left out, I suppose, as a matter ⌣_
a way this is a kind of encouragement. There seems _
have been something like an enduring consensus, re-
flected in our dictionaries, that there are some words so
abusive when seen in print, so cursed and cursing, as
not to be acceptable on a page. It is somehow a different
matter to shout the word, or to hear it spoken; we can
put up with that as we must. But we are not obliged to
look at it.

I rather like that in us.

But, as a footnote, it should be noted that the OED
in its dignity has long permitted the word on its pages
disguised as a bird. The WINDFUCKER is another name
for the kestrel, and earned its name by the grace and
ease with which it hovers, up and down, over the waves.

17

CUPID, VAPID etc.

CUPIDITY is a lovely (love-like) word, a *nizdo*, bird's nest of a word, telling more about love than you wanted to hear. There, nested up in front of your eyes, is the god himself, half fat baby with toy bow and arrow, kewpie, half late-twentieth-century politician, loving and loving, most of all wanting. Cupid was placed there by the language, located precisely in a linguistic cul-de-sac, inevitably forming the word CUPIDITY with its unique, inescapable message. Or perhaps it was not so after all, maybe the language didn't give it as much deliberate thought as I am crediting it with. It could have happened, I suppose, that Cupid and its roots had been hanging around in the language for centuries, never usefully enough employed, and one day, the language thought impatiently, Well, it's got to go somewhere sooner or later, let's stick it into CUPIDITY and give it a try. No matter, it worked, a masterstroke of artisanry, wasting nothing, preserving the meaning of the root and

Cupid, Vapid etc.

the most antique cognates, back to the beginning. At some point, the name Cupid was invented by a Roman committee casting about for a translation of the Greek Eros. Although the language itself decides on the admissibility of all other words, committees get to choose the names for gods. This time it was a very foolish — or a very wise — committee, sunk in cynicism.

The IE root was *kwep*, or *kup*, meaning cook, smoke, move violently, to be agitated emotionally. Something near to the boil, close to burning on the stove. Just the word for building the notion of a particular kind of desire, and it entered Sanskrit as *kapyati*, angry and excited. Old Slavic placed it in *kypati*, to boil. Greek had *kapros*, meaning smoke, getting no further. At last, Latin did what the language had in mind all along and constructed *cupido*, meaning a longing desire, especially for power, and *cupiditas* signifying ambition, avarice, and *Cupid*, the fat boy with his golden and lead arrows and pink skin like porcelain, the root of which, appropriately, is *porko* (an etymological accident: *porko* became the ceramic because of the resemblance of the cowrie shell to porcelain, and because that ridge on the cowrie reminded the language, in its vulgarity, of the backside of a pig, and the image lingers in the person of Cupid).

Cupid had been Eros for the Greeks, but nobody seems to know where *Eros*, as a word, came from. There is no attested root, and all we know of the meaning lies in the various fables circling the central myth of love. Eros was, in any event, a somewhat ambiguous figure. He was, to be sure, the god of love, and a very ancient god indeed, having been born among the first great gods, fashioned from the primal Egg, floating on Chaos, by Time. He was also the son of Aphrodite, later Venus. His principal occupation was shooting his darts into the bosoms of both gods and men, causing endless confusion and some of the most disheartening stories in all literature. He spent an abnormally long time in childhood, which troubled his mother, who fixed matters by producing a second child named Anteros, after whose appearance Eros increased rapidly in size and strength, but never beyond adolescence. His most famous contribution to fable was his affair with Psyche, in which his behavior is open to question: after sleeping with this attractive girl for some nights, he unfeelingly sent her packing on grounds that she held a lamp to get a close look at him in the dark. Psyche was then subjected to a series of preposterous trials contrived by his mother. No thanks to Cupid the couple finally married and produced a daughter named Pleasure, as hard to believe as anything in the long record of mythology.

In all of this there is nothing to explain the basis for any connection of Cupid to CUPIDITY, unless the meaning of love, sexual love at that, is somehow thought to be contained in the kind of desire contained in the root *kwep*. This seems unlikely, even allowing for the seething, violent emotions experienced at times by young lovers. The etymological fault is more likely attributable to the Latin translators who first sought a word equivalent to Eros. Although rootless, there is in Eros no trace of the notion of the avaricious, ambitious, power-seeking young man of affairs whose baby image surfaces in the twentieth-century mind (especially that mind) on encountering the word CUPIDITY.

Maybe the language does get things wrong, really wrong, from time to time, after all. Cupid seems to have been a rather silly mistake.

But there is another way to think about Cupid and his name. He surely was, despite the attested fact that he held high rank among the gods, being well-born and early in his appearance in the pantheon, a rather trivial sort of deity. Although he presented himself as the representation of love, he never became a serious man in any of the great myths, nor had his predecessor Eros much affected deep Greek thought. Perhaps we should be looking elsewhere among the descendants of the IE root *kwep* for a substitute for Cupid, eliminating the literal connection to cupidity. There are at least two candidates, each emerging in Latin from an alternate, extended root *kwap*. One is *vapor*, from Old French *vapour*, Latin *vapor*, steam, not a likely prospect now that I think on it. The other, Latin *vapidus*, is the one I would choose as the alternate for Cupid, without destroying the image. VAPID, the Roman and modern god of love? For these days, it will have to do. It would have been better to have held on to *Eros*, strong enough to provide at least one healthy offspring, EROTIC, although limited to that.

Anyway, the language has evolved a string of stronger, more solid words for loving, and we have little need for Cupid. Casting all the way back to the more

substantial IE root *leubh*, containing the general sense
of loving, desiring and caring all at once, the Germanic
tongues evolved *bileafa*, meaning BELIEF and FAITH,
strong terms indeed and surely the underpinnings of
genuine love. It needed only a suffix to become Old English *lufu*, and then LOVE. Latin used the same root for
libere and *libet*, carrying signals of pleasure, goodwill,
freedom and candor. *Libido* was a more carefully used
variant, cautiously indicating strong desire with risks of
caprice and immoderation, even lust, brushing against
Cupid and cupidity. Sanskrit had *lubhyati*, he desires,
Lithuanian still carries *liaupse* from the same root, a
song of praise. *Leubh* survives in modern German *Liebe*,
solid, enduring love. Light-heartedly, the English LIVE-
LONG DAY comes from the antique original *leof-long*,
dear long day, matching the German *die liebe lange
Nacht*, the dear long night.

The French *je t'aime*, irreplaceable, and all the variants of *amour* emerging from the Latin *amo*, as robust
a source for passionate love as the language has devised,
can only be tracked as far as the ancient Latin word
amma, believed to be a childhood term at the outset.
From *amma* we have the Latin and French words for
love, and also *amicus*, a friend, a reminder not to lose
sight of the old connection between love and friendship.
Also two of the most agreeable English words in the language: AMIABLE and AMICABLE. Not to mention AM-
ITY, a long way from CUPIDITY.

It is as though the language tried several paths into
the meaning of love, then thought twice and corrected
itself. *Kwep* and *kwap* turned out to be the wrong way

Cupid, Vapid etc.

to go, blind alleys leading to CUPID and VAPID. The other roots produced the real idea, the foundation of lasting love: trust, belief, reliance, freedom and desire all combined, something to grow up with, a string of lovely, lovable words.

18

CIVILITY, SULLEN etc.

Hidden deep inside CIVILITY, one of the friendliest words in the language, is the IE root *kei*, carrying along the instructions given by its first meanings in the language: "to lie down; bed, couch, night's lodging, home; beloved, dear." We are, at our best, CIVIL creatures. This is what we mean when we assert that we are CIVILIZED, and when groups of us fail to meet our moral standard, the word UNCIVILIZED is brought in for heaviest condemnation or, when we are talking of primitive tribal societies, contempt.

CIVILITY is an irresistibly attractive word, implying good nature all round, quiet speech, willingness to accommodate and compromise, peaceableness. CIVIL should carry the same meaning, sometimes does ("He's a civil man"), but can be used in violence ("Keep a civil tongue, will you?"). CIVIC is less friendly, more formal, with legal undercurrents.

There is something of domesticity in all these cognates, and no wonder. Our English word HOME can be tracked back through German tongues to *kei*, also HAMLET, also HIDE (the Old English measure of the amount of land suitable for one free family and its dependents). And one of the most domestic of all words emerged from *kei* by way of the Greek *koiman*, to put to sleep: CEMETERY. Also, appropriately enough from the same root, HAUNT.

SULLEN is a word that might be turned to use for describing the problem of cities that fail. Starting as IE *swe*, self, it became *solus* in Latin, meaning alone, then moved to Middle English as *soleyn*, someone unique and singular. But later, when the language had had enough of solitariness and compulsive individualism, *soleyn* came to mean unfriendly, averse to society, morose, and the word became SULLEN.

The language has mixed feelings about the withdrawal of loners. LONELY is a nice example; a lonely person is in a hard predicament, intolerable when loneliness is sustained for long periods. The word itself needs no footnotes; it contains its own feeling of compassion. You would never use lonely in any sense of disapproval.

ALONE and LONE are somehow different. The language distances itself with these words, even though they are built from the same root as lonely. ALONE is *all* plus *oino*, ONE. LONELY is simply a modification of the same root, but somehow changed by the suffix to engage the language suddenly in pity.

But the language feels otherwise about the deliberate, purposeful detachment from society, and has figured out ways to indicate strong disapproval by assigning new meaning to some of the words suggesting isolation. IN-SOLENCE is such a word. When it was first pieced together in Latin, *insolens* meant contrary to custom, unusual, maybe something like quaint; *insolentia* meant not being accustomed to a thing, inexperience. Later on, as the word moved from Latin to the posterity languages, it picked up the pejorative sense of haughtiness, arrogance, bad behavior.

IDIOT had a comparable history, starting out to mean a unique, special, isolated person, ending up in modern English as an even worse term than insolent, an *idiot.*

ALOOF has its own ambiguity, a surprising word borrowed from *luff,* the windward side of a sailing vessel, then used for the now obsolete nautical word *aloufe!,* steer into the wind! Somehow, it moved into its current meaning of standing at a distance, withdrawn, for better or worse. Something moving near to incivility.

The surprise is CITY. Sometimes the language must surprise itself, and then set to worrying over not having got things quite right. Although surely it had the correct expectations early on, being perhaps even more prescient than we know. After all, there are some cities in which the cognate words do seem right; you have to quiet the mind first, then look around: CIVILITY is not everywhere, but it does identify a city whenever the arrangement has been worked on hard enough, for a long enough time. I remember Prague for civility, also Zagreb, also Edinburgh. Needing some editing here and there, civility exists in Paris and London. New York will take time.

19

―――

SCRUTINY, FRENETIC, BOTHER, STOP etc.

Each everyday word that we choose, every day, to fit properly in a string of other words is, in itself, a tiny language. Even the simplest phrase, looked at closely, scrutinized as we say, contains so many clusters of meaning that we would be unable to speak or write at all unless we used it automatically, spontaneously, ignoring the individual significances. It would be a physical impossibility to speak if we were biologically obliged, at the same time, to pay attention to the details as we went along. Under close self-scrutiny, word by word, we would all fall off our bicycles.

Take, for example, that easy-looking word SCRU-TINY. We have it in English on loan from the Latin *scrutare*, with the plain meaning of searching through things, rummaging, from another Latin word *scruta:* rags, old things, trash. The Latin can be tracked back thousands of years to our common ancestral language, Indo-European. The root for *scruta* was *skreu*, meaning to cut up something, also a cutting tool. It passed into Germanic as *skraw*, then into Old English as *screawa*, the name for a SHREW, presumably because of the pointed nose, also as *scroud*, a piece of cloth (whence SHROUD). During the same millennia, moving from one posterity language to another, the root *skreu* held on to the notion of cutting something up, separating the parts in some useful way, and so it happened that *scrutilon*, in Old High German, took on the meaning of inquiring into, investigating, with much the sense of today's English SCRUTINY, a long way from *scruta*, the trash pile, but still carrying the same resonances. SCRUTINY involves more than just the act of sorting through public wastebaskets; it signals to the mind that there are things that must be discarded in order to select the most useful ones.

Other sets of words, at first glance unrelated, emerged from the same root. Latin provided *scrupus* and *scrupulus*, a small pebble, later becoming SCRUPLE, the smallest unit of weight for apothecaries, and SCRUPLE with its other meaning, a nice ethical judgment between matters of conscience, SCRUPULOUS.

PHRASE is an innocent-looking word, indicating nothing more complex than the arrangement of a sequence of words making sense. A phrase is a simple piece of speech, an elementary act of grammar. But look inside for the hidden messages.

Obviously, putting together a phrase of language (or for that matter of music) must involve some degree of thinking, so it does not come as a surprise that the word itself is connected to thought, or at least to the brain.

But only indirectly, and by a route leading from one long-ago error to another. The IE root of PHRASE was *gwhren*, with its earliest meaning, to think. The ancient Greeks, and probably their predecessors, had decided that the center of the mind must be located somewhere in the region of the diaphragm, because of a self-evident connection of breathing to thinking. So *gwhren* evolved into *phren*, thinking, and thence to *phrenicus*, the Latin word for the diaphragm. From this start, streams of words concerning thought came along: FRENETIC, FRANTIC, FRENZY, SCHIZOPHRENIA, all connected to the mind, but not, it should be noted, the mind at its best. It was once believed that the phrenic nerve, a long and conspicuous fiber running up through the chest from the diaphragm to the spinal cord high in the neck, represented some sort of connection between the diaphragm and the brain, coupling the seat of the soul to the more mechanical functions of the brain itself. You might have thought that the term *diaphragm* was similarly rooted, from the sound of the last syllable, but the scholars say no: *phragm* comes from the Greek *phrassein*, to fence in, barricade, plus *dia*, across: the wall between the abdomen and the lungs. I once assumed that DIAPHRAGM came from *phrene*, what with the phrenic nerve and all, and I am still dubious. Now *that* word bothers me, but before I can get to it in the array of dictionaries on my desk, I am bothered by BOTHER.

And so it goes: BOTHER, with the sense of troubling, annoying, exists in Irish *bodar* (confused, deaf), Welsh *boddar*, Cornish *bodhar*, and all these from a very old parent root in IE, *guou*, which meant cow dung, manure, excrement, all with exclamation points, signals of irritation, of annoyance, of being bothered.

And DUBIOUS, a wonderfully simple, explicit, unambiguous word, comes from the IE root *dwo*, meaning TWO, indispensable for making other words involving choices between selections: BETWEEN, BETWIXT, BINARY, DOUBLE, DUPLICITY, and, there it is, DUBIOUS and DOUBT, and the German word *Zweifel*, with the same meaning.

So it goes, no end to it, no way of stopping. Any word not only leads to another, it reaches across and drags you over page after page. One more, just one. STOP: from IE *steue*, Greek *stuppe*, a tuft, and Sanskrit *stupa*, crown of head, a tuft, and English STYPTIC, for stopping bleeding, a word first used for the flax employed as a stopper for bottles. But there is disagreement among the comparative philologists; one scholarly group suggests that both STOP and STUPID and all the other cognates arise from the same IE root, *steu:* to beat, push, knock, with cognates STEEPLE, STEEP, STOOP, STUB, STUTTER, STUPENDOUS, STUDENT, STINT, SHTICK. What a way to talk. How do you use a language in which stupid, stupefy, stupendous and obtend are all the cousin cognates of words with the dignity of student, studious, studio and study? Well, you think about what you are saying, and about what lies behind the words, that's how. Sanskrit *tudsti* means to pound; Latin *studium* had eagerness and zeal for its meaning, while Greek used the same old root to make *tumpenon*, a drum.

ZEAL came from IE *ya*, meaning arousal. In Greek

Scrutiny, Frenetic, Bother, Stop etc.

zelos denoted fervor, *zelotes* were ZEALOTS, so were the militant Jews who resisted the Romans in Palestine. Today it is a word used in academic, military and religious circles, with JEALOUS as the only surviving cognate of ZEALOUS, both words now competing for the same meaning.

20

LUCK, HAPPY, LOSS etc.

It is often remarked that the human mind is unique
among the thinking systems of the animal kingdom because of its capacity to look ahead and commit its long
thoughts to the future. Other animals, it is said, cannot
do this; they live their lives in the immediate present,
making use of memory — which they do possess, it is
conceded — but only for essentially mindless matters
like remembering where to find food or what hurt when
last encountered, certainly not for creating images from
the past to foretell what may happen next year. What
might happen five minutes from now is, of course, a
different matter. Our Abyssinian cat James knows better
than we do when we will be moving from one chair to
another, and is infallibly in our chosen place before the
move, but he has no idea about tomorrow's appointment
at the vet.

Even so, our talent for thinking ahead and making
long-term predictions is never flawless. Things tend to

Luck, Happy, Loss etc.

turn out differently, from time to time we make the wrong guesses, we are obliged to take chances. In the end, we are lucky or not.

The simple word LUCK, always being turned over somewhere in the back of our minds during most waking hours, must have been in the language for as long as speech itself, but its origins are surprisingly hazy, none farther back than Middle Dutch *luc* and Middle High German *gelucke.* There doesn't seem to be any IE root carrying the meaning of plain good luck, except perhaps *kob,* to succeed, providing us with HAPPEN and HAPPY. The notion of bad luck certainly does exist in the IE root *leu,* proposed by some as a candidate (but not attested, and argued over). *Leu* had the meaning to divide, loosen, cut apart, and is clearly the source of our LOSE, LOSS and LOOSE. In Germanic it acquired a prefix, denoting rejection (*far,* from *per*) becoming *far-leusan,* a total loss, FORLORN. In latin *leu* served, with its sense of loosening and disintegration, for the old-fashioned term for syphilis, LUES, bad luck indeed.

Another cited possibility for luck, good luck, is the root *lau,* meaning gain, profit. It is the source of Latin *lucrum,* and our words LUCRATIVE and LUCRE. The moral misgivings in the language about lucre (filthy lucre) are very old; my Latin dictionary gives two meanings for *lucrum:* (1) gain, profit, advantage, (2) avarice. (The opposite of *lucrum* is *damnum,* loss.) This is surely the basis for the sort of luck gamblers depend on and live for, but it is something rather less than what the rest of us have in mind when we think of our chances, of being lucky or unlucky in our lives.

Et Cetera, Et Cetera

CHANCE and CHANCINESS may be better words than luck for this aspect of living. Luck does, after all, carry the vague sense of something to be sought for, worked at; I'd better get lucky, luck out, we say, turning alert. There seems less of an active role for us to be playing with a word like CHANCE; we get it or not, no doing of ours. A game of CHANCE seems to my mind a bit different from one of LUCK.

CHANCE comes to us from the root *kad*, to fall. One of the cognates, CADENCE, carries a piece of the deep meaning for my mind: fortune rising and falling, in a rhythm of its own, and the chance of being lucky or unlucky caught up in the same cycles, beyond control. An unexpected inheritance, a bright guess in science, the wrong subway car to be in, a meteorite heading this way, not really good luck or bad luck, just CHANCE. *Kad* also provides, appropriately, ACCIDENT and IN-CIDENT, DECAY and CADAVER, all falling and befalling. For everyday, ordinary times of unnoticed risk, an OC-CASION, things might befall, fortune might turn, or not.

FORTUNE itself is an old word with a knot of meanings inside: a windfall of money, a friendly nod from the goddess Fortune, *fors* and *fortis* in Latin, luck. The IE root, if any, is not known.

It is self-evident that to play the odds, to be lucky, to win, one must make a GUESS. This is from an IE root *ghend*, originally meaning to seize, take. It carried success in its earliest cognates, as in Old Norse *geta*, to GET. It became *forgietan* in Old English, to lose one's hold, and thus FORGET. In Germanic it formed *getison*, to try to get, in Middle English *gessen*, and then in English

GUESS. *Ghend* also became the source of *prendere* in Latin, to get hold of, and *prendre* in French, and by this route English obtained PRIZE, ENTERPRISE, SURPRISE, all lucky things, but also PRISON and REPRISAL. You take your chances, guessing.

The element of pure chance in human affairs now extends to the universe at large, in physics and cosmology. Determinism departed with a wave as the twentieth century came in, and even biology must now deal with the effects of indeterminacy and randomness. One thing that used to lead always to another now does so only if the initial conditions are arranged in a sameness that is unimaginable, down to the last atomic particle. Probability now governs. Randomness is the controlling urgency in nature. So, it is of interest to take a look at some of the words needed for thinking about the matter, about MATTER itself. The IE root is, expectedly, *mater*, from which we have Old English *modar*, thence MOTHER, MATRIX and METROPOLIS; because of MATRIX and its origins in tree trunks, the language produced MATERIAL and MATTER.

How did we get all the distance from *mater* to MATRIX? Easy, it seems. A modern MATRIX is a form enclosing something that fits precisely inside, a mold or die, or more abstractly, a mathematical array of numerical quantities arranged in a rectangle. But the first English matrix, borrowed from the Old French *matrice*, was a womb. Before that, *matrix* in Latin was a breeding animal, bringing forth something perfectly molded.

Randomness, the central business of matter, came from the root *rei*, meaning first to flow, then RUN.

Et Cetera, Et Cetera

Running at great speed became *randun* and *randum* in Old French, adding the notion of impetuosity and disorder to the velocity. The word appeared in Middle English as *randum,* and began to acquire the sense of uncontrollability and unpredictability, RANDOMNESS. Centuries later, when writers felt the need for a better word for totally random numbers and events, a word was borrowed from Greek *stochastikos,* meaning much the same thing but carrying also the notion of guessing and conjecturing. *Stochastikos* has a long history, beginning with the IE root *stegh,* which had the sparse meaning of something pointed, sharp, perhaps stuck in the ground. The Greeks used the root for *stokhos,* a stake or (later) pillar used as the target for archers. It is a splendid example of the wit and wisdom of the language, and as well a good-humored reminder by language itself, to all its speakers, of the intrinsic fallibility of human endeavor. Archers aiming at a target, even the best of world-class archers, have to rely on good luck. Moreover, they are obliged in their craft, what with wind currents and the odd twitching of muscles at wrong moments, to do a considerable amount of guessing. So it happened that *stochazesthai* carried three meanings at once: to aim at a target, to hit the target, and to guess. The third survived, and STOCHASTIC, referring to random and conjectural events in mathematics, chemistry and physics, is now an indispensable term in science.

Pokorny lists *argu* as the IE root for ARROW, also the source of Latin *arcus,* the bow, and our ARCHER. But there is another root carrying the sense of sharpness, piercing, off on a separate path through the language: *steig*, from which we inherit the names of two creatures needing careful handling, STICKLEBACK, the spring fish, and TIGER. The sharp root for TIGER has been with us a long time; Avestan used *steig* to make *tigra*, Greek *tigris*, presumably because of the animal's most spectacular features: teeth, and speed. Incidentally, we now have a useful slang word, SHTICK, borrowed from Yiddish, based on the same root, for indicating any sort of special talent — like the jaws of a tiger, or a gift for telling pointed jokes.

JOSS, a word for a Chinese idol, is also widely used in parts of the Orient for luck. "He has good joss" is high praise for someone who prospers, also suggesting that he's a good fellow to be around. "Bad joss" is a bit worse than bad luck; there is the added sense that the luck is somehow ordained. It comes from the IE root *deiw*, to shine, producing progenies like DEITY, DIVINE, JUPITER and, much later, JOSS, with the root holding firm.

When bad luck begins to turn up with more frequency than we like, we tend to look about sharply for things to blame. A vast domain of human superstition, including complex rites and ceremonials, is squarely based on the notion that something, a person or a thing, will bring bad luck if not attended to. There is also a general belief that something will happen to good luck if it is not accepted in good grace; a celebration, especially if celebrated too early, can be a bad omen.

So it is nice that language has provided us with an

etymological accident, pure coincidence, that tells us this lesson in a single, short root, *yu. Yu* was an outcry of joy, giving us the word JUBILATION. At the same time, it became the name of a bird prominent in superstition, the wry-neck, otherwise known as the JINX.

21

——

MACARONIC VERSE etc.

English belongs to the Germanic branch of the family
of Indo-European languages, and the lineage shows itself most conspicuously in the numberless words we inherit from our Anglo-Saxon-speaking forebears. It is
odd that so few words of Latin entered the language
during the four centuries of Roman occupation; *castra*,
a camp, became the English town Chester, *caseus* provided cheese, *portus* port, not many others. The Saxons,
centuries before moving to Britain, had picked up some
Latin words in their contacts with the Romans and
brought them along (*vallum*, WALL, *calx*, CHALK,
strata, STREET). Latin was the language of the Church
in Britain since the sixth century. The Norman occupation brought a great tangle of French words to the
language, many of them derived in the first place from
ancestral Latin terms. But Latin itself, now sprayed
everywhere in English prose, entered the language much

later, beginning in the medieval years when the classics were just at the beginning of their rediscovery in Britain.

How did it happen that today's English owes so much to its Latin vocabulary? Great strings of Latin words were picked up, altered to take on an English sound, and then, seemingly effortlessly, embedded in the language. By the sixteenth century, Latin itself had become a second language in intellectual circles; John Locke's *Essays* were written in Latin, later translated into English.

One way it may have happened at the outset is suggested by the abundance of medieval English poems, passed along by the reciters, the oral poets, whose verses were remembered and published later, after the development of printing. Many of these poems are classed under the technical title *macaronic*, from the rustic-Italian *macarone*, meaning a mixture of things. A nice example (taken from Brian Stone's translation in the *Penguin Medieval English Verse*) is a Nativity Poem:

Holy Mary, mother mild,
   Mater salutaris,   (Mother of salvation)
Fairest flower of any field
   vere nuncuparis   (you are truly called)
With Jesus Christ you were with child;
You drive me from my musings wild
   Potente,   (powerfully)
Which make me go to death, I know,
   Repente   (suddenly)

Macaronic Verse etc.

It is startling to recognize the unfamiliar meaning of *Repente* in this context, and similar surprises abound elsewhere in the verses. *Repens* is "suddenly, in a hurry, unexpected." REPENTANT would have needed *paenitens*, as my Cassells only now instructs me.

But this is surely the best of all ways to introduce new words from a different language into everyday speech. Rely on the poets, the rhapsodists. Once they have done their work, the language is transformed, and words like TRANSMOGRIFICATION (probably a cooked word, mixing Latin terms for transmigration and metamorphosis to indicate a grotesque sort of transformation) come easily and happily to the tongue.

Repente seems out of place somehow. I can't help thinking that the writer, whoever he was, had intended to be dying repentant and got his Latin wrong, although not at all spoiling his poem by doing so. There is a connection of some kind between dying in a hurry and being sorry at the end. It is an easy connection in twentieth-century American English, "Oh sorry!" we keep saying to each other all day long, bustling along the sidewalks, jostling our way into subways, "Oh sorry! Oh sorry!" we say. Translated literally, the words mean, "I'm in a hurry!" *Repente!*

Which reminds me of the nice expression in the Chinese language meaning too much of a hurry: *Zou-ma guan-hua. Zou* is to go or ride, *ma* is a horse, *guan* is looking at, *hua* is flowers. To be trying to observe flowers while galloping on horseback is to be sorry. It is startling how often a literal translation of Chinese into English turns into a small poem.

22

—

DIPLOMA

All recipients of honorary degrees should know that those rolled-up scrolls they are handed are not real diplomas, not in any proper etymological sense. The word DIPLOMA comes, simply and by definition, from *duo*, two; a diploma was a sheet of paper folded double. It may be undiplomatic at this late date to raise doubts about such occasions, but it should also be reported that the degree itself is a dubious distinction. From the Latin *degredior*, taken from *gradior*, to step, but now specifying the direction. DEGREE is an embarrassingly close cognate of DEGRADE.

But avoid all such ceremonies, unless you're sure they are the real thing. The Latin *caerimonia* means sacred event, associated with holy awe and reverence. Not a time to be given an unfolded diploma and invited to take another step down.

23

CHILDREN AND LANGUAGE

The earth is filled with talk, but in a very limited sense. Only humans, so far as we know, have evolved a system of communication that allows us to tell other humans everything that is going on in our minds; we have been saying this to each other, over and over again, in all our different languages, and it must therefore be true. Other creatures have ways of communicating with each other, sending clear and explicit messages, but never with the subtlety and complexity of human speech. But perhaps some of the messages represent the rudiments of language; perhaps the gift of something like speech has been selected for in the evolution of all species and only we humans, thus far, have broken through and emerged with metaphor as our sign of triumph. Dolphins make sounds that seem to be messages beyond our comprehension, whales sing deep mysterious songs to each other across undersea miles. Fireflies congregate by the millions in tropical trees, flashing together in absolute

synchrony for the marking of species ready for mating.
Crickets chirp in tight rhythms, each identifying family
members keeping in touch; when the weather chills
down, the male crickets chirp at a slower rate so pre-
dictably that farmers and naturalists can make accurate
guesses at the temperature change. It is a comfort to
know that the female's receptor apparatus accommo-
dates by slowing accordingly. Sometimes the messages
are sent across species lines: the honeyguide is a small
African bird that locates honeybee hives in forest trees
and, by a seemingly deliberate, specialized call, signals
the exact location to the human beings who follow the
bird and then break open the hives, leaving behind am-
ple supplies for the birds' needs.

The communication devices of other animals differ
from our human messages to each other in fundamental
ways. They are, necessarily, direct unambiguous signals:
"We are here, ready for whatever, willing. Come. Go.
Look out. Danger!" There is no time or need for our
sort of ambiguity and redundancy. Telling a lie has no
part in the information strategy, as it does with us. Although I should mention the report by an entomologist
studying fireflies that the females of one species have
been observed to signal the flash sequence of a remotely
related species, thereupon attracting a male of the latter
line, and thereupon eating him. Being human, awash in
ambiguities, I was shocked to read this account.

Children are the best of all at language. They begin
learning speech in the first two years of life, and proceed
through an almost stereotyped series of stages, lasting
for several years, during which they pick up grammar,

Children and Language

word order, syntax, inflections, all the rules. Most of us believe that children learn to speak because their mothers teach them the language, but it may not be so, any more than fathers teach them to walk by dandling them from their fingers from room to room. Walking is simply done, when the time comes to walk, and so it is with talking. There are reasons to believe that children arrive at the age of two already in possession of the neural mechanism for making grammar, and then they make use of whatever human sounds they hear to make their own language. Noam Chomsky developed the notion of an embedded *bioprogram* for speech, switched on in early childhood for language acquisition. Switched off in adulthood, I'd guess: I'll never in my life learn to speak French convincingly, having tried too late in life. Derek Bickerton, studying the emergence of Creole languages in regions where human communication had been disrupted by colonization, carried the idea still further. Children, Bickerton concludes, are not only spectacularly skilled at acquiring speech, they actually *make* language. His chief example is the development of Hawaiian Creole. In 1876, the sugar import laws in the United States were relaxed, and the plantation industry throughout the Hawaiian islands underwent a rapid expansion. The native Hawaiian population, already diminishing, was nowhere near adequate for the labor needs, and field workers were brought in from China, Japan, Korea, the Philippines, Portugal, Puerto Rico and other places. Within a few years, the islands had become a jumbled polyglot of different tongues, crowded with working people who had no way of comprehending each other. Then, beginning in the 1880s, just as happened in other newly colonized regions of the world in earlier centuries, a pidgin language emerged, pidgin English in this case to accommodate to the dominant language of the occupying power. Strictly speaking, pidgin is not really a language; it is made up of convenient words borrowed from all the available language sources and then strung together in more or less random order. A pidgin can be an effective device for conveying simple directions and pointing out things to be done, but it is not a useful mechanism for conveying ideas of any complexity. For the time being, through the rest of the nineteenth century and up until around 1910, pidgin English served as the working speech for communicating between the groups of newcomers to the islands. But during the same period of a few decades, a completely new language, Hawaiian Creole English, made its appearance and spread through all the communities and plantations. Hawaiian Creole was a genuine language, equipped with its own tight rules of grammar and syntax, made up of words and the roots of words already at hand (many of them English), capable of expressing subtleties and abstract ideas and displaying novel features of grammar not traceable to the rules of any of the existing languages.

Bickerton, in the 1970s, carried out an exhaustive study of the languages used by different age groups and arrived at an astonishing conclusion. Hawaiian Creole was not at all made by the adults in the original immigrant population. Indeed, when the new language appeared and spread into general usage, it could not be understood, much less spoken, by the older adults. Bickerton concludes that Hawaiian Creole, a brand-new, independent, free-standing, proper language, must have been put together, built from scratch so to speak, by the children.

If Bickerton is right, we have a new possibility to consider in speculations about the origin of human language, whenever it was that that landmark event for the species took place. We are born — or at least our species since Cro-Magnon man thirty-six thousand–odd years ago has been born — with centers of some kind in our brains for formulating grammar and manufacturing metaphors. Moreover, we become specialized for this uniquely human function in the early years of our childhood, perhaps losing the mechanism as we mature. This might account for the other peculiar and paradoxical feature of our species — the very long period of time that we spend in immaturity and physical vulnerability. No other species remain for so much of their lifespan as defenseless children. Perhaps we do so because that is the period in which our brains are so immensely productive for the survival and further development of our species, learning to speak and acquiring new ideas about acquiring ideas.

24

━━━

PUPIL, FOCUS, MUSCLE etc.

A PUPIL, the word for a young student, was used in fourteenth-century English as the legal term *pupille*, for an orphan child, a ward, and it is so recorded in the 1382 Wycliffe Bible. Two centuries later a pupil was simply a young student. In Old French, the word was also *pupille*, taken from Latin *pupus* and *pupa*, boy and girl. *Pupus* may have come from an IE root *pap*, meaning a nipple, or from *pau*, something small (from which the French *peu* and our word FEW).

But the word PUPIL is also used for the clear dark center of the eye through which light penetrates to the retina. However does it happen that the same word names a small child, off to school, and the pupil of the eye?

Both PUPILS can be tracked together far back in Latin and beyond into IE, although the IE root remains uncertain. The naming of the pupil of the eye has been widely attributed to the reflection of a very small person, which is seen when one looks closely into the eye of another. In fact, the OED cites a now-obsolete phrase, "to look babies," used in several seventeenth-century writings to describe this close kind of visual contact.

It seems a fair guess that this use of the word PUPIL was an invention of young children. Who else would even spend the time required, scrutinizing another human eye, and would then conclude that the reflection is itself a small child? It is also a safe enough guess that the eyes being examined usually belonged to mothers. To provide a clear enough reflection, the looker must be very close up, but should also be looking into a relaxed eye with a dilated pupil, the sort of eye mothers can best provide when sitting in domestic peace, child on lap, the mother preferably not concentrating directly on the child's own eye but more likely thinking of something else, off in the future. A focused eye, inches away from a larger, unfocused eye, is the best circumstance for perceiving the pupil in the pupil of the eye, and a small child is the best witness to be engaged in such a business, and the likeliest to name the image.

There are lots of other words, now dignified by long usage among adults, that could well have received one or another of their early meanings in a child's mind. FOCUS itself is a nice example, to my way of thinking. Originally, in Old Latin, FOCUS meant fireplace, hearth; it became *focalia* in Vulgar Latin, *fouaille* in Old French, and FUEL in English, always with the meaning of fire. But the hearth was also the center of the household, the place where all domestic activities converged, and the word took on its other senses, ranging from

FOCUS as the center of interest to the FOCAL point in optical systems to which light rays converge. It is this kind of connection between familiar aspects of a household and more abstract affairs in the world outside that children are good at perceiving. Poets too, but then poets are what they are, in part anyway, because they succeed in retaining the genius of a childhood mind. Only a child would have used the root for a MOUSE, *mus,* to make the word for MUSCLE, probably because of the way a flexed biceps appears.

This won't do, of course. If the extensions of PUPUS are to be attributed to the children among us, the same could be said for words like HUMANE and HUMANITY arising from the word signifying the earth and its stuff, *humus,* or the word TRUTH in its tour from *deru,* something solid, to tree, to true. Still, it is just as hard to credit all the rest of us, adults fully versed in whatever language, with the good sense to agree on assigning new and profound meanings to whatever old words happen to be lying around. Children, at least, have the advantage of always wanting, by some sort of social instinct, to be *at* each other with speech, all day long, all night if possible. And they have plenty of time on their hands, childhood being the peculiar combination of leisure and incessant social activity that it has always been.

Or perhaps we adults have really, without realizing it, brought language along to its present distance (nothing near to what it may eventually become), simply by adding more and more of ourselves to the participants. Maybe it requires a certain density of the population to begin making language, and then, the more speakers, the more inventive and metaphorical the speech. After all, thirty-six thousand years ago there were probably no more than a few human beings of today's variety occupying the entire planet. Most of this tiny population were spread across the vast area of central and northern Africa, too sparse a company to form real villages, perhaps only nomadic families here and there, and no time for settling down for conversations around the fire.

But then, perhaps around the time when Cro-Magnon art began its development, language and speech may have been launched. Now there were settlements, encampments, the beginnings of agricultural communities, plenty to talk about and enough people to do the necessary talking. Most especially, enough children, crowded. I can imagine how a language may have started, but I cannot guess at how the first speaking children ever managed to teach this new thing to the elders.

It may have happened in another way, and I cannot prove it, but I cannot think of another way. A friend told me a story about a visit she made one afternoon to the public library, at a time when a nature class for young children was in progress. Among the displays was a caged live owl, and the children were assembled around the cage close up, transfigured by interest. Suddenly the owl's nictitating membranes crossed the eyes, covering them, while the eyelids remained open, then recrossed again. The teacher was equally excited, and asked the children, "Now what was that? What did it do? What would you call that?" There was a long silence, and then one small boy said, voice rising, "Windshield wiper?" It is not quite a story of a child inventing a new word, but surely one about finding a new use for an old one.

25

NEANDERTHALS, CRO-MAGNONS
etc.

Our immediate predecessors,* perhaps our forebears, more likely distant cousins, were the Neanderthals, first appearing around one hundred twenty thousand years ago, in sparse settlements in Germany's Neander Valley. Most specimens postdate seventy-five thousand years and the last Neanderthals existed around forty thousand years ago. No evidence can be found of a genuine culture beyond crude hand stone tools (no handles or hafts), and signs of the use of fire and burial of their dead. They had bigger brains than ours, but no likelihood of language. Perhaps a larger brain needs editing, as occurs in all human embryos. A larger birth canal in Neanderthal does suggest large newborn brains, which in the circumstance could be a disadvantage. In the modern human embryo, great numbers of cells, neurons and

*White, Randall. *Dark Caves, Bright Visions: Life in Ice Age Europe.* New York: The American Museum of Natural History and W. W. Norton & Co., 1986.

Et Cetera, Et Cetera

their circuits are put in place, partially interwired, then ruthlessly edited away, on a massive scale, and replaced by others in accordance with the new genetic instructions. The survivor cells at the end of the process may actually be sparser than the populations destroyed in the course of redesigning and rewiring. Neanderthal's adult brain may have been too gross, unpruned, overwired, thus still speechless and muscle-bound.

Also, early childhood, the time when our proper species is at its brightest and best for learning language, may have been a very different and probably shorter period for Neanderthal. It has been estimated from measurements of the birth canal (based on the structure of pelvic bones), that gestation was much longer, twelve or thirteen months, and the size of the newborn brain correspondingly larger. This could mean that less time was available for further development and expansion of the brain. The Neanderthal central nervous system may have been more elaborately fixed in place prenatally, leaving a significantly shorter postnatal period for further growth and remodeling, not sufficiently flexible for new masses of cells or new diagrams of wiring. The early months of infancy may thus have lacked time for environmental stimuli to have their effect on the neural adaptation required for speech and the comprehension of speech.

Never mind, for the moment, the more ancient evolutionary leaps and the questions they raise: which gorilla-like or chimpanzee-like or baboon-like (or human-like) is our likeliest (or most likable) ancestor? Only one huge evolutionary event, earthshaking as it was to turn out, concerns us here: the transition from a sort-of-human species like Neanderthal, unable to speak in today's meaning of language, to a talking, comprehending, totally new nervous creature possessed of words and grammar.

Neanderthal was hardly what you might expect in a species destined to dominate a whole planet, and as it turned out he did not. But just to look at him, in his museum reconstructions, standing in front of the cave, his chances would have seemed considerably better than ours. He had enormous shoulders, huge muscles, heavy bones, a cavernous skull case. But he missed, lasted only eighty thousand years, then vanished into time. What did he lack? Not, as has been suggested, the *physical* capacity for speech — it has been an old, accepted notion that Neanderthal's brain was big enough for language but he had the wrong set of pharyngeal and laryngeal structures, preventing the enunciating of all the consonants and vowels at our disposal. This is nonsense; we have speechless people today, deaf, mute, discussing the world eloquently with only their hands for sign language. Anyway, the anatomical defect is not the explanation, according to a recent archaeological group which studied, with close care, a typical Neanderthal dating back around forty thousand years, well-preserved.* This ancient man's hyoid bone, a technical necessity for the human larynx, was precisely the same structure, in the same location, as our modern speech

*B. Arensburg et al. "A Middle Paleolithic Human Hyoid Bone." *Nature*, 338 (1989):758–760.

organ, as were the other bony points for the attachment of all the muscles needed for the articulation of words, any words. In short, Neanderthal could have spoken at length, if he'd known how to speak or what to say. His brain, big as it was, did not yet contain the needed wiring instructions for making language. And because of this lack, Neanderthal lost his way and vanished in the ice and snows of forty millennia ago.

Then we came up, naked, hairless, clawless, near toothless for predation, vulnerable, even innocent-looking when viewed close-up. But the pure sound of the strings of words we could make set us up for survival, then dominance.

Language is what preserved us. Not because it does real damage to any other species, but because we can use it together. It binds us, unites us, can join hundreds, thousands, now billions of us together to make a single tremendous creature: a social species.

The gift of speech led straight on to another outcome, the added gift of friendship, even affection.

Left to ourselves, untroubled by the anomalous few among us who have tended inexplicably and unluckily to become our leaders, folly after folly, we do indeed like each other, often enough *love* each other. It is a biological necessity, looked at objectively, if you hope to work your way through evolution as a social species. We haven't found our way yet to this kind of safety, but give us a few more centuries.

Cro-Magnon man was a new phenomenon in nature, so separate and different from Neanderthal as to seem a new species.

Neanderthals, Cro-Magnons, etc.

Anatomically indistinguishable from today's human being, the new people were spectacularly (and aesthetically) an improvement. New, inventive tools with handles were produced and then steadily improved. Weaving, rope-making, tailored clothes of a sort (from fabric and skins) appeared, along with fishhooks, fishline, sinkers. Harpoons, spears, bows and arrows.

They left the signs of long-distance travel, probably trade. Certainly, there was much more success in population and survival, more dense communities, more niches occupied, whole continents occupied; watercraft was a certainty. Exploration and colonization thrived. South America, long believed to have been inhabited by humans only eleven thousand years ago, now displays some evidence indicating settlements as far back as thirty-five thousand years.

Art arrived in the human mind with the Cro-Magnons, leaving its evidence in rock paintings, ornaments, jewels, sculpture and musical instruments (flutes, rattles). They had a long run at life, surviving to sixty or more. This must have affected biological success and improved the survival of whole populations. Older citizens can be assets for survival, providing a steady cohort of experienced, savvy minds. And better survival for the old also means, almost inevitably, better survival all round and therefore more children. It is hard to imagine the sudden emergence of all these social activities, especially the evidences of art, without imagining language as well to make the rest possible. Once we learned this, we could spread around.

And spread we did indeed. In only thirty-six

thousand—odd years (many of them very odd, and very cold) we have occupied every part of the earth's surface, hostile or not, increased from a few hundred thousand to five billion and still counting. No such biological explosion has ever happened before — not even the distinguished, all extinct trilobites, unaccountably almost everywhere, can match the spread of humanity. We are still swarming, talking and talking.

26

HAIR etc.

Whenever it was that we achieved speech, working together on this new hard thing, and, along with language, became conscious of others, then ourselves, and then, everything ready, began assembling in small groups for conversations, what on earth did we talk about? The world at large in all its strangeness, I'd guess, and then the most urgent particulars. One thing we must have noticed, early on, was HAIR, and I am confident that we talked a lot about that. I don't suppose that our peculiar near-hairlessness was necessarily an embarrassment, but it was a plain fact that virtually all other creatures in the wilderness were hairy, many of them dangerous (bears were so feared that the IE root *bher*, BEAR, is believed to have been taboo in northern Europe; the animal was "the BROWN one"), and there we stood, upright, opposing our thumbs, brainy as all get-out, but bare-naked.

We still retain HIRSUTE from an IE root for hairiness,

ghres, from which words with a bristling meaning have descended: GORSE and sea-URCHIN, for example. The inner feeling of apprehension holds in the more common cognates: HORROR, HORRID, HORRIFY, ABHOR, hairy words for hairy circumstances.

Then, as sometimes happens, the language made a light joke about it. Needing a word for wild impulse, a sudden change of mind, two old roots were combined. *Caput,* head, joined itself to *riccio* (Latin *ericius*), a hedgehog, yielding a metaphor for hair standing on end, CAPRICCIO for that kind of music in Italian, and CAPRICE for hair-raising but rather enlivening behavior in English.

Another IE root for hair is *pilo, pilus* in Latin, a word that could mean a single hair or, in another context, anything trifling. The French called their tough bearded soldiers *poilus,* and the same root provides PLUCK and PILLAGE in English. *Capillus* became the collective hairs on the head, from which, because of their threadlike appearance, we have CAPILLARIES.

The notion of leaping and capering in CAPRICE leads the OED, also Weekley, to the opinion that it derived from the Latin *caper,* a goat. Webster says not so, also the AHD, also Partridge. There are similar disagreements about the hair metaphors involving some other animals. HAREBRAINED sounds right enough for naming a wild and inadequate mind, but, thinking on it, HAIRBRAINED contains the same idea and has been frequently used in English since the sixteenth century. A CATERPILLAR is so named from the Old French *catepelose,* from Latin *catta,* a cat, linked to *pilus,* "a hairy cat," I've no notion why. But the modern French word for a caterpillar is *chenille*, literally "a hairy dog" in its roots. Ah, language.

Meanwhile, we do have that goat in our word CAB, from the French *cabriole*, originally a light coach that tended to leap and caper like a goat, or a New York TAXICAB on a hairy ride in from Kennedy.

NUDE and NAKED both come to us from IE *nogw*, from which we also have the Greek *gumnos*, naked, *gumnazein*, to train naked, and our GYMNASIUM. I've never heard the words applied to any animal but humans, with two exceptions: *The Naked Ape*, a book by the anthropologist Desmond Morris (about us), and a breed of mice useful in immunological research called nude mice, again because of hairlessness. You've never heard of a naked bear. Even a highly trained chimpanzee, working away at sign language, performing brilliantly without his jacket and pants, would not be thought of as nude. *Nogw*, I believe, had its first meaning as hairless, clothes or no clothes.

27

GOOD, LEARNING, JULY etc.

For all our embarrassing present flaws as a species, we represent, just for having survived this far, a stunning success. More than this, a success in the face of one near-lethal adversity after another. Within an infinitesimal fraction of geologic time, we came to life as a total novelty, covered almost the entire surface of the earth and in the same moment, like it or not, began to manage its affairs, sitting atop the biosphere as no other creature has ever done before. We did that through a series of catastrophic ice ages that must have killed off any number of other much older, larger and stronger contemporaries.

The most recent ice ages, eleven of them in succession, starting around twenty-five thousand years ago, must have played a central role in our social evolution. Some of the stretches of dead cold over what had been temperate zones lasted as long as twenty-five hundred years, others only five hundred. They came to an end, at least for the time being, some ten thousand years ago. During that period, the Upper Paleolithic, our species was subjected to a pulsatile instability of climate that must have exerted enormous selective pressures on each cluster of generations. We would have had a thousand years or so of benign temperate climate, with abundant sources of plant and animal food, then two thousand years of deep freeze, then another warming followed by a freeze. Eleven cycles. Fifty generations of humans would learn to adapt to one kind of world, a reasonably friendly one, only to discover that completely new rules for survival would be needed for the next fifty generations. Darwin's famous term "survival of the fittest" must have applied more stringently and successfully to human beings within this brief evolutionary period than to the numerous other species that vanished from sight. It is a safe guess that two human attributes had the greatest demands placed on them: intelligence, first of all, and skill at social living, which is obviously an aspect of intelligence. The response, saving us all, was speech.

Grammar, as a neurological problem, is relatively simple, just waiting for the right questions. But the hard puzzle, the core of the matter, is something else: how do you make up the words to use once you have all the syntax in hand, all ready for speech? What do you say?

I cannot believe in a neural center for words, not anyway in the central nervous system of any solitary human being. Words, as I see them, can only be put together by the jabbering of humans gathered together finally agreeing, for example, that words for TOGETHER and

GATHERING in Indo-European speech should also be connected to another word meaning GOOD. Or that the word to be used for learning something new, *mendh* for instance, would fit nicely some day into the predictable but still unreachable word MATHEMATICS when the time came for that.

Language is itself the most exhilarating of games, an endless contest in which we are engaged all our lives, pure fun for the mind. It can be, at its best, a game infinitely more complex than chess, or at other times athletic, world-class soccer, team against team. If you say blackberries are red when they are green, it is like tossing a light ball easily caught.

Another person's mind is the most engrossing of all the puzzles in the world. This is what first catches the attention of children from the moment speech begins to take hold. Earlier in infancy the mind seems totally preoccupied by the most personal needs: food, warmth, comfort, the mother. But with speech at hand the child begins paying close attention to the world around, which means people, all needing to explain themselves. Tell me why, the child says with his first words — not why any particular phenomenon but why everything? Why you? Why the world? What are you thinking? Tell me the world.

Finding out is an endless game. Whatever the first words actually seem to be saying, the first urgent message — to parents, sisters and brothers, visitors, strangers on the sidewalk, the family dog — is "Think with me." And, once begun, this becomes life's mission for almost all of us, surely all but the most unlucky. "Think with me" is what we really mean when we use the term *consciousness*. When we say that we are conscious, we do not intend to say something important about the workings of our own brains, we are talking, etymologically, about the minds of others. And this, of course, is what the language intended. Consciousness is knowing together. So, for that matter, is *conscience*.

It is often asserted by authoritative scholars, most of them scientists, that evolution has to be purposeless in order to work, that randomness is the law, and that progress, therefore, is an impossible notion in accounting for human affairs. Each culture, it is asserted, is the previous culture with transient embellishments, one thing after another, but never up or down, only the same old human behavior. No real, lasting ups; downs from time to time, like now: if you are looking around for improvements in human living you have only to take a look at the twentieth century to see that we are hardly on a level, sinking really. Do not hope for progress; we haven't seen signs of it yet, we never will.

I disagree, tentatively. Some very good things have happened to our lives, just in the last few centuries, that could have been guessed at, wished for, maybe not predicted as such, but hoped for in some certainty.

Everyone says there is no such thing as a primitive language, and on the evidence this is so. The languages studied by professional linguists in isolated tribes of hunter-gatherers in deep Africa, or among the aborigines in Australia, or the speech of Eskimos and the native Indians of North and South America are fully as complex and subtle, as tightly regulated by syntactical

rules, sometimes containing many more grammatical inflections than modern English or French. To search
among these tongues for evidences of "early" language
development, as was once the hope of linguists, is to look
in the wrong place. And any search for other evidences
of fundamental features of human language, language
in general, a universal structure underlying all forms of
speech, while still hoped for by some linguists, is still
(while not hopeless) beyond reach.

So we are left with no good clues that lead to any
revelation of the earliest origins of speech. In short, no
one has a glimmer of an idea what the first speakers had
to say to each other, as long ago as the origin of art in
Cro-Magnon communities. Still, there must have been,
at some time in the deep past, a very beginning of language, and it very likely started as a primitive scheme
for communication, needing time and effort — probably
a very long time — for its evolution and development.
Perhaps, after all, we do observe something vaguely like
its origin and growth in those regular and predictable
stages of acquisition of language by young children, just
as earlier on we can see traces of the development of our
ancient biological origins in the maturation of the human embryo.

We take for granted that there was once an ancestral
tongue that comprised the origin of almost all modern
languages in Western civilization, but proto–Indo-
European itself seems to have been a fully formed language, no less sophisticated and flexible for its needs
than any of its progeny. This being so, we are obliged

Good, Learning, July etc.

to imagine the existence of a still earlier speech, or a set and series of still more antique languages. After all, the dates of Indo-European culture are quite unknown, but probably extend back not much farther than eight thousand years. Very likely, the antecedents of Chinese go back just as far, maybe longer ago.

Languages do not die, not ever. When we speak of "dead" languages, we really mean forms of speech, like Latin or Sanskrit, that evolved into offspring languages. It is the most natural of processes, affecting as it does every existing language; English is itself a spectacular example, differing as much today from the English spoken in the tenth century as today's French differs from Latin. Words change in their form and outer meaning, new words are made by patching together strings of older words; old words in any language disappear, of course, over and over again, but they tend to spring alive again, looking like something else.

I shall now tell a story on my grandson, two going on three, for he is busy learning language and has just in the last few weeks, under the direct influence of being toilet-trained by his parents, made an entirely new and highly useful word. And all on his own. Like all children of his age his speech is vulgar, still unconsciously so but vulgar anyway. He goes *peepee*, sometimes just *pee*, and on occasion, using his potty, he goes *poopoo* (never *poo*). He may well have picked these up from his parents and friends, likely so. But the great event is using these primitive roots to make his own new word, employed for the general information of the world around that he is now,

Et Cetera, Et Cetera

on his potty, doing both at the same time. His new word is *poopee,* which his parents and grandparents regard as a masterpiece of economy and unambiguity, and, as well, an unmistakable early evidence of linguistic brilliance still to come.

28

GOOGOL

All modern dictionaries carry the word GOOGOL, short-hand for a very big number, 10^{100}, a one followed by a hundred zeros. A GOOGOLPLEX is almost infinitely bigger, a ten raised to the power of a googol, more zeros than I can think of, 10^{googol}.

These are among the newest of words, and their entry into the language, or anyway into the dictionaries, is so recent that everyone can rely on the story of the original coinage, no need to guess. It is a nice story, making its own point. In Kasner and Newman's 1940 *Mathematics,* the American mathematician Edward Kasner writes that he asked his nine-year-old nephew to think of a name for a number with one hundred zeros, and the boy promptly said GOOGOL. No one tells us why, and I suggest a need for new scholarship. Barnhart proposes an association with the comic-strip character Barney Google, but this doesn't satisfy me. I think of *goggle-eyed,* but I don't know, any more than I can imagine

Et Cetera, Et Cetera

where or how or why any word in the language made
its very first appearance. There are of course lots of
words pieced together from other standing words, the
necessary jargon of professionals in one field or another;
the computer scientists are inventing whole lexicons of
their own — but these strike me as code words, even as
small blueprints, not language in the flesh so to say.

29

DIGNITY, DAINTY, WAR etc.

A *doublet* is the technical term for one of a pair of words that derived from the same original root and then came up through the language by different routes of transmission, meaning quite different things.

DIGNITY and DAINTY are textbook examples, having emerged from the IE roote *dek*, with the assigned meaning to take or accept, with the added sense of something fitting and respectable.

The words that we have in English from *dek* are remarkably consistent with the charge contained in the root. The Latin *decere*, to be fitting (and acceptable), became our English word DECENT, as fitting a word of approbation as any term in the language. *Docere* in Latin, from the same root, now meaning to cause to accept, or to teach, became DOCTOR, DOCENT, DOCTRINE, and, with a gently pejorative shift away from such strong cognates, DOCILE. The Greek word *dokein*, to cause to be accepted, was taken into English as

DOGMA, ORTHODOX and PARADOX. *Discere*, to learn, provided DISCIPLE and DISCIPLINE. Latin *decus*, an ornament, became our DECORATION. And *dignus* in Latin, meaning fitting and proper, yielded DIGNITY and DAINTY, the doublets.

DAINTY seems wildly removed from the meaning of DIGNITY, looking like a sort of linguistic accident. But in Middle English it was *deinte*, borrowed from Old French *deintie*, meaning something not only fitting but extremely pleasant, delicious, not all that great a distance from the worthiness of the Latin *dignus*. Even today, centuries later, DAINTY has, for all its daintiness, a solid core of value; it is, as the dictionaries say, something "delicately beautiful, charming, exquisite." It is not as light a word as it seems on its surface. In its own way, DAINTY carries itself with a certain DIGNITY, after all.

Another pair listed as doublets are the terms HOST and GUEST, both coming from the same IE root *ghosti*. In modern English, these are of course completely different words in sound as well as meaning, opposites in fact, but for many centuries the predecessors of HOST and GUEST were much more alike, reflecting the intuitive obligation in earlier cultures, particularly nomadic societies, to provide not only courtesy but hospitality to a stranger.

The stranger, in Old Germanic language, was a HOST (and from time to time the word has been used to mean enemy, even an army of enemies), but he was at the same time another sort of host, a person receiving another as his GUEST. The ecclesiastic HOST comes from

Dignity, Dainty, War etc.

Latin *hostia*, victim, sacrifice. On the other hand, the GUEST (in old English *gaest*, Old Icelandic *gestr*) was a stranger, sometimes an enemy, and yet the term *guest* described a person invited in. The ambiguity is not much clarified by a glance at the other cognates derived from *ghosti* (ghost, by the way, is not one of them; it comes from a different IE root *gheis*, from which we also have ghastly). In addition to GUEST and HOST, *ghosti* is the root in HOSTILE and HOSPICE, and of course HOSPITAL. It wandered long ago into Slavic; the Russians say *Gospodin* for sir and master, and *goss* for both an alien and a guest. We are instructed by the host-guest reversible meanings that we are a hospitable, generous species, always hopeful but worried by long, careful memories. The *xeno* in xenophobia has recently been proposed as a cognate of *ghosti*.

The doublet for NOISE is NAUSEA, and both derive from the IE root *nau*, simply a boat, NAUTICAL. There is ambiguity here, even a touch of wit, especially when you read the modern physicist's definition of noise: "any disturbance, especially a random and persistent disturbance, that obscures the clarity or quality of a signal," as indirect and delicate a description of sea-sickness as you could ask for.

A venal sin is unforgivable; it is the selling of one's services or influence basely. It contrasts sharply and sometimes confusingly with a VENIAL sin, which is by definition forgivable and based on affection; the two words are not doublets, for sure. The root *wes*, originally to buy or sell something, produced VENAL, also VEND. Selling seems to have been a questionable way to make a living, as far back as the words go; the Latin *venditatis* meant putting something up for sale, and the word for the seller, *venditator*, had the meaning of boaster, vaunter. As for selling oneself, VENALITY has been an English synonym for corruption for at least four centuries.

Despite the sound resemblance, venial has no connection to venal, comes from a separate root, *wen*, and concerns a totally different human activity. *Wen* meant to desire, wish for, and although it generated the name of the goddess of love as well as several cognates referring to sexual love, its principal progeny were important words for ambition in general. VENUS, of course, is associated with VENERY and VENEREAL, nothing much to be done about that, also, paradoxically, VENOM. The latter seems to have resulted from the unskilled pharmacology of ancient people who prepared "love potions" for those in need. It must have been a risky sort of drink, whatever it was they put in it, since it not only produced our word VENOM but also caused another root, *po*, to drink, to become the origin of two English words that would not otherwise be etymologically linked: POTION and POISON. Latin *venenum* could mean a drug, a poison, a love potion, a dye or just rouge, depending on the context.

Wen-ya, meaning favor, went into Latin as *venia*, forgiveness, hence VENIAL, a gentle attitude toward sinning. Gentler still are the cognates VENERATE and VENERABLE, carrying the root for affection, love and wishing to a new level, respect.

SCANDAL and SLANDER, although quite different today, are doublets of a sort. They both began in the IE

root *skand,* meaning to leap or climb, providing us with
ASCEND, DESCEND, also TRANSCEND, also climbing by
ladders, ESCALADE. Behind the notion of leaping and
climbing is an obvious associated idea for worrying humans, and there it is in the Greek *skandalon,* a stumbling block, a trap. It is still there today, buried inside
the other cognate indicating entrapment: SLANDER. But
how did these words suggesting a snare emerge together? *Scandalum,* in Late Latin, was a temptation, a
trap, then took two separate but related paths. Old
French had *scandaliser,* leading to Middle French *scan-
dale,* signifying irreligious conduct, a discredit to the
church, and this was its meaning when borrowed for
English SCANDAL in the sixteenth century. Old French
also had *sclaundre,* meaning defamation, injury to
reputation, which appeared in Middle English as a scan-
dalous report, a SLANDER. Dr. Johnson's eighteenth-
century dictionary lists slander and scandal as verbs,
both meaning "to censure (or charge) falsely."

The root *wers,* meaning to confuse, led to two cognates differing only in degree, accompanied by just one
additional word, nicely qualified to serve as a doublet.
The first two are WORSE and WORST; the third is WAR.
This is one of the shortest and perhaps oldest language
lessons in the language.

30

FREE, FRIEND, COMITY etc.

Sanskrit dictionaries list several words for loving, arranged in order of both intensity and degree of attachment. *Snehah* meant fondness, *anurahah* implied devotion, while *manmathah* was reserved for passionate and presumably sexual commitment. *Priyate* simply meant to love someone, and *priya* was the word for dearest, beloved. The words are etymologically distinct from one another, but linked directly to the IE root *pri*, meaning love. *Pri* had at its outset only the single meaning of love, but later, in Old English, the words became *freo* and *freond*, providing modern English with both FREE and FRIEND, both still with a half-buried sense of loving, or at least affection.

Another word for preference, much thinner and less committed than loving and its cognates, is LIKE. We say we like so-and-so, or such-and-such, meaning something like friendship and a mild wish, but with a reversible sense always there in case. Old English *lician*, and Gothic *leikan* meant to please. Oddly, the same IE root, *lik*, is the origin of the pleasing sort of LIKE, and also of LIKE when used in its sense of something similar, alike, and the LIKE that is partly cut away at the ends of words and replaced by -ly. Lively, for instance, was live-like, likely was like-like, lovely was assuredly love-like. LIKE is still useful, in some contexts indispensable, but nothing like as heavy a word as love and the cousins of love. It implies a kind of choice when the odds favor that choice in the mind, but always the option of withdrawal if it turns out not to one's liking. I like this-or-that, for the present; tomorrow we can think again. Or, tossed in front of friendly sentences: "Like wow!"; "Like it's raining." Or tossed behind, as in an OED example from a 1966 magazine: "C'est la vie, like!"

The word COMITY, used particularly to describe a relationship of friendship among countries, as in "the comity of nations," has been in common use since the sixteenth century. It is not quite affection, but it does something more than refer to peaceful, nonaggressive intentions; it has somewhat the nicer sound of liking. It is at the same time two sentiments, a stronger yet milder feeling about the national attitude involved. In order to earn the merit of the term, countries must be displaying something more than general goodwill, something less than the strictures of formal peace treaties. A 1543 reference (Becon, in OED) cites "honest behavior, affability" along with COMITY as ideals for international connection. But considering the size, complexity and innate unpredictability of whole nations, it is a word of genuine power and force.

Et Cetera, Et Cetera

It is, I think, the word COMITY itself, and its IE root, that gives the flavor. Nestled comfortably, the meaning is hidden in the *mity* fragment of the word, preceded by the old root *kom*, together (forming *kosmis*, later the latin *comis*). The *mi* comes straight from IE *smei*, and Sanskrit *smi* and *smitam*, which meant simply to smile. COMITY is, literally, the accomplishment of nations smiling together; perhaps even more than this, smiling *at* each other. There are no laws of international behavior here, no sanctions, no signatures of heads of state on sealed documents, only the general good-humor implied by that smile. It has been a rare, maybe in fact nonexistent phenomenon in the modern history of nation-states, but the term exists handily, something devoutly to be wished for, now more than ever.

Smei is one of the loveliest and liveliest of all the old roots, and has been evoked with taste and consistency down the ages. In English we have MIRACLE and MARVEL as direct descendants, also ADMIRE, all smiling. Latin contained *mirus*, wonderful, and *mirari*, to be amazed. The wonder at a MIRAGE must have been associated with pleasure at the sight. A reflecting glass surface may have taken its name MIRROR (forms of which existed in Old and Middle English) when a child was engaged, smiling at himself, observing his own face for the first time, very likely naming the surface himself. It is the sort of thing I would expect a young child to do with language, just one among a great many.

31

EVIL, WORSE, WURST etc.

The language tends to extremes in its view of human
morality, leaving any middle ground hard to locate
among the words for behavior. It is sometimes near to
Manichaean; actions and intentions are either altogether
good or irretrievably bad, not much in between. With so
many roots available for indicating the quality of life,
the dualism seems strangely unbalanced. There are a lot
more unequivocal IE roots for good words than bad,
counting them up. The language evidently has a preference for displaying our admirable aspect, although the
scattered terms it reserves for disapproval are potent.

EVIL, for instance, had to be contrived as a word
rather late on; there seems to be no IE root as an at-
testable antecedent. *Upo* has been proposed as a candidate, but it carried only the meaning of "up from
under," with its other related descendants lacking any
discernible link to evil — UP, OPEN, OFTEN, OPAL.
Later, a Germanic word, *ubilaz,* appeared meaning evil,

listed by Pokorny as a derivative of the root *upo*, but still being argued over. In any case, *ubilaz* is accepted as the source of *yfel* in Old English and EVIL today. Our word VILE, strong as it is, has no known IE root; we have it from Latin *vilis*, where it meant nothing more than cheap, of no value.

The root *dus* had the meaning of bad, evil, but only because it later could become the prefix for an array of quite nice words, thus turning their meaning around. *Dus* attached to *ease* became DISEASE. Thus also DYS-FUNCTION, DYSPHORIA (reversing euphoria), DIS-GUST, DISTASTE, DISGRACE, DISSONANCE. No longer nice, still not strong enough words for real evil.

The word DIRE may have been a try in the right direction, but turned instead into something fearful, even horrible, but not wicked. DIRE came from the IE root *dwei*, to fear, into Greek as *deinos*, fearful, into English as DINOSAUR, the fearsome lizard. It is nice to know that *dwei* is closely related to the root *dwo*, two, from which we have DOUBT and DUBIOUS, being of two minds, the direst of human predicaments.

Another IE root, *wer*, meaning turning, bending, provided a few condemnatory words for modern English, but these seem to have turned up almost by accident along with a cascade of other words with quite different meanings. *Wer* was the source of WRONG, PERVERSION and SUBVERSION, not really approaching evil, and also turned out unimpeachable words like WORTH and STALWART, perhaps from the "inward, toward, equivalent" senses, and VERSE, WRINKLE and WORM, from the turning, bending notion. A separate root, *wers*, mentioned earlier, began with the meaning of mixing up, confusing things, and evolved into WAR, WORSE and WORST, but then fell away from the effort and produced the sausage WURST (an ambiguity again, by definition).

INHUMAN and INHUMANE are as strong terms for evil as you are likely to find in the language. For our instruction, they carry the message, reassuringly, that the *normal* behavior of humans is HUMANE behavior.

Gwhen, an IE root meaning to strike, kill, yielded Old English *bana,* a slayer, and modern BANE and BANE-FUL, clearly connected with evil. But the same root, perhaps because of being used for hacking through the woods to make a path, produced the blameless, baneless AUTOBAHN.

BALEFUL certainly has undertones of evil, and is derived from the IE root *bhelu,* which meant to harm, ruin. It became *balu,* ruin, in Old English, and BALE, an evil influence, in modern English, but with no other related cognates.

It is a surprisingly short list, considering the almost unlimited scope for the varieties of human behavior that we could all agree to condemn. But there it is, the vocabulary is unbalanced, our terms for evil are vastly outnumbered by the words we use to felicitate ourselves.

An English lit major once told me that when you count up all the words repeated in Shakespeare's plays, the most frequently used is GOOD. It comes from a solidly attested IE root, *ghedh,* meaning uniting, fitting, with cognates TOGETHER and GATHER, as you might expect from a social species. BETTER and BEST came from a separate root, *bhad,* which despite its bad sound meant unqualifiedly, good. *Bhad* led to *betera* in Old English, BETTER, and *betest*, BEST. It also turned up in Old Norse as *batna* meaning to improve, from which we took BATTEN (we kept the sense of improving, but regrettably it took on an added sense of doing so at someone else's expense).

Although there are only a few IE roots with the direct meaning of evil, there are many indicating bad behavior — striking, beating, cutting and so on — but these do not necessarily imply other humans as the objects of striking. There is a good deal of optimism about the human condition in the IE lexicon, and a surprisingly high appraisal of behavior itself. Indeed, BEHAVIOR is a word testifying to good nature. The word assumes goodness. We do not qualify behavior unless it is in one way or another reproachable. Parents instruct their children: "Behave," or "Behave yourself." If that doesn't work, the admonition will take the form of something like "Stop behaving so badly." *Behave!* means something more than *conform! do as the rest of us do!* It means, simply, *be decent* (another good word, from IE *dek*, to accept, with cognates DIGNIFY, DECOROUS and DISCIPLINE). It means *be human!* It means, in an earlier sense, *happen!* Oddly, BEHAVE has no direct IE counterpart, it is a manufactured word with a root bearing no semantic link: *kap*, merely to grasp, producing Old English *habban*, to HAVE. Latin *capere*, from the same root, handed along such words as CAPABLE, CATCH, ACCEPT, PERCEIVE. Germanic took *kap* for *bihof* for that which binds, and it moved to Old English as *behofian*, to have need of, and BEHOOVE, usually meaning you'd better behave if you want something good to happen.

Gene and *bheu* are the most prolific roots for assessing human behavior. *Gene*, meaning simply to become, beget, with offspring like KIN, and GENIUS, gives us KINDLY and KINDNESS, GENEROSITY and BENIGN, GENTLE and GENIAL. *Bheu*, signifying being, existing, growing, became the root for nature at large and ourselves at the same time: PHYSICS, and, for our encouragement, FUTURE. We have manufactured words for evil by turning some of the *gene* and *bheu* cognates around, attaching negative signs: MALIGN, UNKIND, BONDAGE. BEING and EXISTING, the oldest of riddles for humans to contemplate, are notions embedded in other roots. The strangest, for the turns it took through the language, is *es*, to be, from which, as we have seen, emerged the English words IS (French *être*) and, to our surprise, YES. While it was still part of IE speech, *es* was suffixed and became *esu*, meaning *good*, and *esu* became EU, the prefix for all sorts of antique good words: EU-DEMONIA (Aristotle's term for happiness in a rational life), EULOGIZE (extol), EUPEPSIS (a good digestion), EUPHEMISM (the use of good words to hide bad ones), EUPHORIA (feeling good). The easy transition from IS to YES to EU is another example of the built-in hopefulness, whatever the odds, in the language.

Deu is another nice root, self-congratulating. From an earliest meaning of doing, showing favor, it multiplied in the language: from *dw-enos* to Latin *bonus* it turned into BONUS, BONANZA and DEBONAIR. Latin *bene* provided BENEFIT and BENEVOLENT. *Bellus*,

pretty and fine, became BEAUTY, BEAU and EMBEL-
LISH, even BEATITUDE. Greek had *dunasthai* from *deu*,
to be capable, and from this we made DYNAMITE, currently used on Columbus Avenue for approving a kind
of chocolate cake.

The language exhibits a benevolent tolerance for the
development of words whose close connection is not ev-
ident at first glance. Who could have predicted that our
words OLD and ELDEST would share the same root as
ADOLESCENCE? The IE root is *al*, meaning to grow,
nourish, providing words as seemingly different but sub-
tly connected as ALTITUDE, EXHALT and ADULT,
ALUMNUS and ALIMONY. Another root for growing is
aug, to increase, giving AUGMENT and AUGUST,
AUTHOR and AUCTION, EKE and NICKNAME (originally
an ekename in Middle English, an added name, then,
carelessly, *a nekename*). The word GROW itself came
from *ghre*, which produced, in the best of worlds, GREEN
and GRASS.

In the end, the language makes the judgment of behavior, formed by speech itself. Ordinary human behavior is taken for granted, expected. Bad behavior,
egregious, out of the fold, is an unexpected thing, an
anomaly, attributable to a defect in nature. Thus, the IE
root *mei*, with only the meaning of changing, moving
from one place to another, has given us MISS, AMISS
and MISTAKE, from the Germanic derivative *missjan*,
to go wrong. The same root provides MEAN, MEAN-
SPIRITED, indicating miserliness, cruelty, malice: a
mean man. Incidentally, and accidentally, there are two

other identical words meaning totally different things: the medium, average person, representing the MEAN (from IE *medyo,* middle), and the MEAN meaning to define or denote (from IE *mei-no,* opinion). But the third MEAN means *mean, mean,* MEAN.

32

ACCIDIE, ANOMIE etc.

To be a surviving pedestrian on the sidewalks of New York City takes special skill and training. The problems are not so much those encountered at busy crossings, when agility and speed and an instinct for avoiding outright death are usually enough to get you through. It is the seemingly simple act of walking along the sidewalk, threading your way through the moving crowds of people coming at you from the opposite direction, that poses the harder puzzle. The worst of possible outcomes is the mutual embarrassment involved in the standoff, when two individuals advancing toward one another try to move quickly out of each other's way in synchrony, and find themselves either bumping or trapped in a sidewise dance. The way to avoid this, I have learned, is to avoid the eyes of the oncoming pedestrian. If he, or she, catches your eye, both of you are at risk. If you really look at each other, full in the eyes, even at some distance away, you can be certain of colliding regardless of footwork. Each of you needs to have the other somewhere in the field of vision, but never in the center of the field. If you can learn to keep every member of the approaching crowd off somewhere at the outermost corner of your eye, something not much more than a moving object occluding the light, you'll have no trouble. Automatically, by a series of instantaneous reflexes, you and your stranger will pass each other neatly and without notice.

I have learned this lesson only recently, having noticed that there are many more people walking much more rapidly on the sidewalks of my city, and I'm pleased with my discovery. But having made it, it now occurs to me that a closely related problem, *reading*, reading anything at all, newspapers to the *Encyclopaedia Britannica*, has similar problems, maybe solved by the same technique.

Never look a word straight in the eye, especially one that you've just noticed there at the end of the line you're on, even one standing out a paragraph down. Do not engage the word, or you will be brought to a standstill, wordless.

Some words, in particular, should be held off from eye contact right up to the last moment, glanced at only in the instant before you pass them by, moving along the sentence. If you can see them coming, it may already be too late. There they will be, staring you in the eye, blocking the way. By then it is too late, you will be immobilized, dead in your tracks, even done with reading.

Two such words, in my own experience, should be kept in mind, or out of mind. They are ACCIDIE and ANOMIE. Neither of these is likely to be encountered in

the course of a normal day's reading. The statistical
probability of running into both on the same page is
vanishingly small, but such things can happen. Never-
theless, singly, each will turn up every once in a while,
there at the end of a line of other words, loaded.

Everyone should be prepared for ACCIDIE and AN-
OMIE, in case. They cannot be ignored, or walked
around. They fill the path, and they do not move.

ACCIDIE has been in the language since the Middle
Ages, and in classical Greek, as *akedos,* much longer
ago. Its literal meaning is not-caring, but the IE root was
kad, sorrow, hatred; *kad* is the origin of our word HATE.
ACCIDIE was used in vernacular for a while for slothful,
surely a misreading of its real intent. It is a word dark-
ened from within, as are few others, and it contains lay-
ers of significance that can be quickly inserted as a fixed
disturbance in a reader's mind. It speaks of an old, enduring flaw in human nature, living without emotion,
without sorrow or hatred or love, a condition of the
mind that should worry the species by its very presence
in the language. If ever turned loose, spreading from the
occasional change of mood in one or another single mind
out to the population at large, ACCIDIE could unseam
society, reducing institutions and governments to standing empty ruins. There it is, in and out of one mind and
another, in and out of the language, something like an
evil wish. Withdraw, it says. Never mind, it repeats. Let
the world go, it says. The hell with it, it says, and once
said and truly meant, so it becomes. What happens if it
spreads? What if a whole society became afflicted with
ACCIDIE?

Accidie, Anomie etc.

ACCIDIE is not so much a description of a state of mind, it is, in itself, a feeling. It could almost serve, in a word, as a suicide note. It has moved nearer to the surface in this century than in earlier times, I think, not as a result of all the wars and seizures of the collective mind but as the cause. It is the opposite of affection, and at the same time the opposite of hatred. The world is not worth the trouble, ACCIDIE says.

ANOMIE is even worse. Do not look at this word. It pretends to mean lawless, but it says much more in a low, expressionless voice. It withdraws, looks into the distance, ignores, feels nothing. ANOMIE exists in the human mind, as in the language, as a kind of latent contagion.

Boredom itself is a rootless word that means more than it says. Boredom at large, generalized, is a deadly serious affair, for which the term is a euphemism hiding malignity. It was put more candidly in the borrowed French word *ennui*, before that word took on airs and assumed its languid, modern air. ENNUI, really a tough word, comes from the Old French *enui*, straight from the Latin *in odio*, in hate. If ever a whole society were to become afflicted by ENNUI, or ACCIDIE or ANOMIE, all the meanings of the word SOCIETY would vanish overnight.

Taken together, ACCIDIE and ANOMIE, and ENNUI as well, are expressions of the deepest kind of sadness that can afflict a society. Fend them off; look away. And remember what SADNESS really means, as it comes down the sentence staring at you. The IE root is *sa*, meaning satisfy, satiety, to have enough, and then, telling us more than we know about ourselves, SAD.

33

EXCLAMATION! etc.

Any writer of prose should be compelled, by law if necessary, to submit professional credentials and undergo a waiting period of seven days before placing an exclamation point at the end of a sentence. Writers of poetry are automatically excluded from such use, almost by definition. There may be occasions when an exclamation point is excusable, perhaps even justified, in certain kinds of writing — public street signs, for example, like STOP!, DANGER!, TERRIBLE DOG!, but not among the sentences of any ordinary paragraph.

The problem is that once you allow one or two in, they tend to multiply, scattering themselves everywhere, expostulating, sounding off, making believe that phrases have a significance beyond what the words themselves are struggling to say. They irritate the eyes. They are, as well, pretentious, self-indulgent and in the end almost always pointless. If a string of words is designed to be

an astonishment, a veritable terror of a string, the words
should be crafted to stand on their own, not forced to
jump up and down by an exclamation point at the end
like a Toyota salesman on TV.

My earliest realization that these marks simply cannot carry weight came on a day years ago when I encountered, in a learned essay on the language of African
Bushmen, the name of the language and its speakers:
!Kung. My first reaction, involuntarily, was to wonder
what there could be of such surprise in the word *Kung*
to warrant sticking the exclamation point in front instead of behind. Then, pulling myself together quickly,
my second thought was anger. Who thought this up?
What linguistic anthropologist commandeered the language, all on his own, and took such a liberty? Who said
he could? I know about the Spanish convention, but at
least they use two, and the one in front is inoffensively
placed upside down. The Greeks used semicolons at the
end of questions. I have no objection to these conven-
tions. But new revisions should, in a better world, be
worked out by international agreement. What would we
all do if words suddenly turned up with semicolons in
front, or periods?

And all that confusion over the clicking sounds used
in the speech of the !Kung Bushmen. Not just the exclamation point, there are bizarre signs for other sounds in
the same tongue (tongue is right) for certain words: a
circle with a dot in the center, indicating a variant click
or cluck, still other marks for the giddy-up sort of
sound. The section in our eleventh edition of the *Bri-*

tannica on Hottentot language goes on and on about these matters, citing early-twentieth-century linguists who got carried away by the speech of Bushmen.

But we should not have to put up with !Kung!

On the other hand, reading about other people's language is a good thing to be doing, even when made grumpy by irritants like !Kung. Something surprising is bound to turn up. Here's a nice thing about the Bushman language. Their word for Bushman, same word for human beings in general, is *koi.* Their word for kind and friendly is *koi-si.* Their word for an especially generous person is *koi-si-b.* And their word for humanity is *koi-si-s.* Clicks and all, their language seems to be carrying the same hunch about the species, human and humane, as we have seen in the Indo-European family. Maybe we should give this an exclamation point!

34

———

MUSIC, CROWD, ABSURD etc.

Music, the most enduring and influential of all our social activities, comes to us from the IE root *men,* from which we derive most of the words for using our minds and thinking. One dictionary definition of the root *men* is "to think, with derivatives referring to various qualities and states of mind and thought," casting the widest of etymological nets. The root for MUSIC comes along in the Greek word *mousa,* a MUSE, in the intellectual company of Avestan *mazda,* all nine of the Greek goddesses of the arts and sciences, the Latin goddess of wisdom, MINERVA, the madwoman attendant of Bacchus, MAENAD, the Avestan spirit AHRIMAN, the German MINNESINGER and the Greek EUMENIDES, mind-users, thinkers all.

We have probably been making music for as long as we have been whole human beings, perhaps longer. For all we know, the Neanderthals may have possessed song of some sort, and an inbuilt sense of rhythm. But we do know that drums and various flute-like instruments first appeared in the earliest Cro-Magnon settlements, thirty thousand years ago, and it is likely that some sort of genuine music emerged along with some sort of language, and we can guess that the art was already well developed by the time of the Indo-Europeans, although there is no way to guess what the sounds were like.

The etymological connection of music to thinking is something to think about. Each activity of the mind is reminiscent of the other. Music at its best, I believe, even at its worst, is a way of telling us how our minds are really working.

No other human social behavior, not even language itself, changes and grows into new complex forms as ungovernably and spontaneously as music. We have records of the details and composition of music for only the most recent period in our thirty-five thousand years of humanity, but what we have seen and heard in those centuries has been an astonishment of change. And although we can trace the influences of one style upon the next in academic ways, we know next to nothing about the changes in the emotional attitudes of our changing societies that made the growth in complexity and meaning of music inevitable. Johann Sebastian Bach turned up in his time, in a family long obsessed by music, and transformed the art all by himself, changing it fundamentally for the centuries ahead, without anyone in his generation, including perhaps himself, realizing what he had done. A whole century passed before the *St. Matthew Passion* was acknowledged as one of the singular human achievements in history, and it is only in the twentieth century that the complete works of Bach have been assembled and played before large audiences. And even now, with the new technologies for recording and broadcasting music, Bach, the master of music at large, is often referred to as the master of baroque, with footnotes in dictionaries attesting that baroque, a highly ornamented style of painting, sculpture and music, got its name from Federico Barocci (1528–1612), an Italian painter who in any case did not paint in the baroque style. It is, by the way, more generally believed that the word came from Portuguese *barroco*, a pearl of strange irregular shape. But Bach is not to be localized in any category.

There is an IE root that continues to perform a useful critical function for certain cranky types of music, some of them currently in fashion, signs of our times, aleatory, minimalist and their expressionless successors. The root is *swer*, meaning to buzz, whisper, probably at the outset an imitative word. It was taken up in the Latin word *surdus*, deaf, mute, then in *absurdus*, with the literal meaning unmelodious, a wrong sound, centuries before moving into English as our stately word ABSURD. We still use SURD for irrational roots of numbers in mathematics. In phonetics, any voiceless sound is a SURD.

It is likely that music has always come in two separate modes, one for participating, the other for listening, and these may have been quite different subjective experiences. Among the early cognates of MUSIC in several languages are words indicating joy and high pleasure, which may have come from the sheer rapture of singing, especially singing with others. Human song has become a branch of language itself. Or could it be the other way round after all, with the words taking on new meanings and messages because of the new tones attached to the words, and the rhythms?

Music made for listening is indeed something different. Whether instruments or human voices make the music, it needs close attention and a silent audience. Yet huge crowds can be assembled to listen to music, and the people will sit, even stand, for hours, concentrating on what they hear, and thinking. Whether they are listening to Bach's *Art of Fugue*, or Mozart's *Don Giovanni*, or the Beethoven Late Quartets, or Brahms or Bartok or Eliot Carter or whatever, the music catches and holds their close attention. What the listeners are doing is thinking about thinking. Music, when it works, is the sound of thought. The individual human brain is an immense living creature made of interacting, interconnected thoughts, moving about in a nonlinear, dynamical system at something near the speed of light, always vulnerable to huge rearrangements and changes in patterns when subjected to minor disturbances in the order of any part of any thought. It might be like the metaphor in the mathematicians' "butterfly effect": the slight disturbance of the air over Shanghai by a butterfly will cause, months later, sustained storms in New York. Music has the power to introduce any number of such disturbances, unpredictably and sequentially, and the result is something like chaos, but a chaos with its own, unpredicted form and order. The pleasure of music is, in part anyway, the unexpected, sustained sense of surprise that it induces in the mind. It is hard to imagine utter surprise as more than a momentary sensation, *on* then *off,* but what profound music does in the receptive, attentive mind is to produce a steady, unwavering high plateau of surprise, lasting as long as the music lasts.

But *chaos* and *unpredictable* and *surprise* are all the wrong words, I know, and we possess no vocabulary to account, even lamely, for the sensation of music. Perhaps this is because we haven't learned enough, or been here long enough, or grown up yet as a species. If this is true, a bright prospect for the millennia just ahead will be to keep on discovering new kinds of music, and comprehending at the same time, with language, what we are really doing inside our minds. We will have become something quite new ourselves, close to what we would be calling a mutation if a change of such dimension were to happen in another species.

For the moment, it remains a mystery. It should be noted that the old root giving rise to mystery was *mu*, with cognates MYSTICAL and MUTE. MYSTERY came from the Greek *muein*, with the meaning of closing the lips, closing the eyes. It has been proposed several times in the past century that mystery and music may be etymologically related; *mu* would have served nicely for both.

35

ETHICS, MORALS, AMBITION etc.

We do not pay much attention to our existence as a social species, and perhaps this is just as well. We tend to think of ourselves as solitary individuals, off on our own in a society made up of five billion or so other single beings, always glancing uneasily at each other, trying to figure out the rules. If we had the biological fact of our existence as social animals always in mind, at the top of our minds, we would feel obliged, from one moment to the next, to be always at work trying to reorganize the ways in which we live together, by new rules, thought up quickly, and things would go wrong. We would form new advisory panels each week to construct elaborate governmental structures, pass laws, establish regulatory agencies, even set up police forces and armies, all obsessively directed at our improvement as social animals, and we would in all likelihood botch things. Some of this we do; it is the way we live these days. Much better *not* to have it in the top of our minds; it is firmly enough embedded in the back of the human head and will organize itself in its own way, given enough time. Right now, because of the noisy triumph of individualism in the last two centuries, and especially because of our collective follies since 1914, we seem to ourselves to have lost the game altogether, on our way to extinction. Good. We will need a few more decades of deep discouragement, casting about for ways to change our behavior toward each other, and then perhaps the notion deep in our collective unconsciousness will take hold, and we will start changing without realizing that we are transforming ourselves. To save ourselves as a species, we need to be doing something quite new, letting nature, at last, take her course, and relying on the language for new guidance.

Social systems like ours, elsewhere in nature, run themselves. The interdependence of bees in hives, or termites in their hills, is nothing like as biologically compulsive as the forces that drive humans into living together.

The language is filled with instructions for getting along in the density of social living. Most of the signs are readily found in the IE roots; some have been linked to other roots in compound words, often still carrying their warnings out on the surface. In many instances, however, the roots are now hidden inside, still alive and pulsating, still delivering their messages.

We have the notion of ETHICS from ourselves, literally

straight from the root, and the root *swe*,* even though vanished from sight, still lives deep inside the word.

The root of MORAL is *me*, "expressing certain qualities of mind." Hence Old English *mod*, Germanic *mothez*, mind, spirit, MOOD, German *gemüt*, *Gemütlichkeit*. Perhaps Latin *mos*, wont, humor, and English MORAL, MORALE and MORES. Also, strange but true, MOROSE.

There are some things that the language prefers not to come right out with, others that it cannot say plainly even by trying. For such circumstances, being beyond embarrassing, the language obscures the deficiency under words designed to hide, or half-hide, the fact that something is hidden.

AMBIGUITY is such a word (from Latin *ambi*, around, plus *agere*, to wander), signifying doubt about something spoken or written, uncertainty about which of multiple meanings the word or sentence (or paragraph — or even whole book) intends to convey. The term often indicates a literary device, something written that way on purpose. The reader is left to pick and choose, hoping to be lucky with the correct meaning, and the critics are happy. The French used the word less ambiguously: *un ambigu* is a meal with everything on

Swe is given in AHD as "pronoun of the third person and reflexive (referring back to the subject of the sentence); further appearing in various forms referring to the social group as an entity, (we our)selves. . . . The extended root *swedh* 'that which is one's own,' peculiarity, custom, led to *swedh-sko*, Latin *suescere*, custom, and Greek *ethos* and *ethic*, custom, disposition, trait."

the table at once, including dessert. In fact, AMBIGUITY is essential in poetry, and it is in poetry that one discovers that the most important pieces of information that humans have to convey to each other all contain double or quadruple meanings.

Ambi happens to be a useful prefix for this function in other contexts. AMBITION, with all its present undercurrents of meaning, some commendable, some lifting the eyebrows just slightly, is itself an ambiguous word. But in Latin *ambitiosus* meant, literally, canvassing for public office, going around shaking hands, gathering votes, an entirely unambiguous, candid word. Another nice *ambi* word was invented by Sir Thomas Brown: AMBISINESTROUS (or AMBILAEVUS), an allusion to ambidextrous, meaning the possession of two left hands, or, in a word, clumsy. AMBIVALENCE is an almost brand-new word, invented in 1910 by the German psychiatrist Eugen Bleuler to mean holding two or more strong ideas about the same object, on the analogy of equivalent. AMBISEXUAL speaks for itself.

A SUBTLETY is something hidden, but there to be got at if you feel for it. It originates in the IE root *teks*, to weave, later *tile*, a covering of some sort. *Subtile* is an earlier variant, with *tile* having the sense of *text*. Something subtle has something in addition lying beneath the text. It is a careful word, to be used sparingly.

An ENIGMA is a linguistic puzzle, maybe a sort of riddle, for which the language is not obligated to provide a solution. Indeed, if a statement is really enigmatic it is likely to stay that way, no matter how often you turn it over for scrutiny. ENIGMA came to its present senses by an unlikely course. The IE root *ai* meant nothing more than something spoken, an utterance, as noncommittal a root as you could hope for. The Greeks suffixed it to make *ainos*, a fable or riddle, and then *ainissesthai*, to speak in riddles obscurely, and *aenigma*, a puzzle. Latin took the identical *aenigma* for mystery, something insoluble, thus our ENIGMA. It does not imply any mistrust or misregard of the language to employ a simple root meaning utterance to build in other tongues a new word meaning fable or puzzle; it is simply an open acknowledgment that this is the way language tends to drift unless closely watched, even *when* closely watched.

PUZZLE has a somewhat similar history, emerging into English from an ambiguous past. The suggested IE root was *paus*, meaning pause. It became *pausa* in Latin, cessation, the end of a process, later in Vulgar Latin *pausare*, meaning to put something in place. *Posen* in Middle English was used to indicate suggesting, proposing, supposing, and POSE itself in its sense of putting a question, asking a riddle. The use of POSE to suggest the riddle itself, or to indicate something beyond explaining — "that's a real poser" — is believed to be the source of the verb *pusle*; in the sixteenth century, meaning to bewilder, confound; thence our PUZZLE, the riddle.

And RIDDLE is another riddle. It may derive from the IE *ar*, fitting together, and thus be cognate with Old English *raedelse* with the meaning of advice or opinion, which would place RIDDLE in the company of our word READ. The oldest meaning of READ was to advise, even to govern (*rede*), and it is hard to make the jump from this to a word like RIDDLE. But perhaps it was a shorter distance in the centuries before writing was a commonplace habit, when reading was an almost magical art, and grammar a mystery.

A LOGOGRIPH is another kind of riddle, usually an anagram in verse. The word itself is more fun than the puzzle: it is *logos*, the word, plus *griphos*, a Greek fishing basket.

The meaning of speech, or writing, can be nicely hinted at, without directly committing a position, by referring to another, more distantly related item of speech or writing. The maneuver is an ALLUSION, indispensably useful in poetry and music but also handy in everyday speech. ALLUSION is itself a lovely, simple word, clear as light. To ALLUDE is, unambiguously, to play with, from Latin *ludus*, a game, *ludere*, to play a game. An ALLUSION is just that, playing the friendliest of games with words. An ILLUSION, by contrast, is not so friendly, and not a fair game. It is deception, the word says so despite the *ludus* root: it is *in* plus *ludus*, playing against the rules. The notion of play in words is a very old one, with the IE root *leid* meaning to play or jest; LUDICROUS is a product.

LUDICROUS is used for things that are genuinely funny, nothing else is hidden in the word, it is a game, fun. It only seems to have some similarity to RIDICULOUS, but you can feel the difference just looking at the two words, they even sound different at their depths. It is, I assert, the roots that have made the difference. *Leud* keeps its place, holding laughter in its word. RIDICULOUS, in contrast, has an IE root *wrizd* governing its inner meaning, and a Sanskrit cognate telling the truth on it: *vridate*, ashamed.

Most of the other words we use for things we wish to conceal in language have transparent components, disclosing the act of hiding. ARCANE language is from *arca*, a chest, coffer, from IE *arek*, ARK, something contained and guarded. ARCANA are words that are secrets, usually unrevealed. CRYPTIC speech is similarly hidden; IE *krau*, *kru* meant concealed, Latin *crypta* was a vault, Greek *kryptos* was hidden. An ABSTRUSE bit of language is *ab* plus *trudere*, words pushed away. RECONDITE speech comes from Latin *recondere*, to put away, store, hide. To say something EQUIVOCALLY is to speak with two voices, avoiding the center, the truth. OBSCURE language is from the IE root *skeu*, a cover, a hide, Latin *obscurus*, concealed away. ESOTERIC words are intended to be understood by a small, elite group, and the word itself is only an elaboration of the Greek *eso*, meaning within, in, inside. OCCULT talk derives from IE *kel*, conceal, cover, save, with cognates like CLANDESTINE, HELMET and CONCEAL itself. An EVASION is from Latin *ex* plus *vadere*, to hasten away, dodge; to EVADE in language is not just walking away, it takes agile footwork. VAMOOSE, by the way, is a cognate of EVASION. DECEPTION is *de* plus *capere*, to snare, to take away. A SUBTERFUGE is *subter* plus *fugere*, to flee secretly, under cover, in the night. When the language wants to dodge, it lets you know.

36

QUANDARY

The dictionaries are in a quandary over QUANDARY. O.o.o., they say: of obscure origin. There ought to be a connection to QUANTITY, maybe QUALITY as well, but they can't find one. The OED, tracking the word back to 1580, cites a guess: from the French *qu'en dirai-je*, what shall I say of it?, then, thank goodness, dismisses that guess. Partridge approves a Latin source: *quam dare*, how much should I give?, or *quando dare*, when to give?, but the perplexity in the dilemma posed by QUANDARY doesn't have much to do with any problem of giving. It is a metaphor describing the mind immobilized by questions, all opposed.

It simply must have derived, somehow, from the IE root *kwo*, the source of most questions about the world. It is a hooting of urgent, usually unanswerable questions. WHO? WHAT? WHERE? WHEN? WHICH? HOW? Then a few automatic, unsatisfying answers from the same root *kwo:* EITHER, NEITHER, NEUTER, ALIBI.

155

Et Cetera, Et Cetera

Then an effort to employ the root to measure the world, or its parts: QUALITY, QUANTITY.

What could be more natural? Given no way out, the language would be simply obliged to slip in a word between QUALITY and QUANTITY, sheltering itself from the blasts of questions coming from all sides, a Roman square of a word: QUANDARY.

37

TRIVIAL, TRIVIA etc.

TRIVIAL is one of the weightiest words in the language, close to imploding under the pressure of all the meanings contained inside, nontrivial. At the beginning, before its long march out of Latin through the Romance languages to its final settlement in British English, it linked two words, one signifying three (IE *trei*) and the other roads, ways (IE *wegh*): the junction of three roads, the TRIVIA. Perhaps on the notion that in any location where three roads meet, people are likely to congregate and talk together of commonplace matters, the weather perhaps, the time of day, the condition of the marketplace, other small views, TRIVIA took on its misleading dismissive trivial sense.

But this was only the least and lightest of meanings, a misinterpretation of the immense role played by smalltalk in keeping societal discourse going. At the same time, the adjectival TRIVIAL grew in latent power and violence into one of the deadliest of imprecations at the language's command. Today, scientists in particular, but other professional thinkers as well, live out their long harried lives in a fear deeply embedded in the backs of their minds that someone, in some public place, will attach the word TRIVIAL to this or that idea or piece of their work. For a published observation to be called TRIVIAL will kill off the prospect of promotion or tenure just as surely as if it were judged as fudged, or derivative, or even swiped. It is almost as bad, but not quite, as fraudulent. The penalty for producing a TRIVIAL finding is not to be brought up on charges, not the assembling of an ethics committee, it is something worse: to be ignored (literally, made not-known).

But then, the word turned in its steps and took on a completely different meaning, or several at once. A TRIVIUM, in the medieval scholastic world, was no small thing. It was the first three branches of the seven liberal arts, lesser but essential, to be got through on the way to knowledge: *grammar, logic* and *rhetoric*. Once these were behind, one could move on to the higher ground of thought, the QUADRIVIUM, *arithmetic, geometry, astronomy* and (at the top, catching the breath) *music!*

Still another turn: the biologists picked up TRIVIAL for its obligatory usage in the classification of animals and plants. The second of the two Latin names is the trivial name, describing a genus in a specific, sometimes vulgar term. *Scolytus destructor* is one of a family of wood-boring beetles; the trivial name specifies the creature for the severity of its ravages. *Mus musculus* has its trivial name from its size: a specifically *little* mouse.

Even the mathematicians found a use for TRIVIAL,

deeply arcane: "a coefficient or other quantity not containing the quantity of the set considered," a definition which all by itself illustrates the indispensability of bare symbols, rather than words, to convey meaning in the language of mathematics.

38

MATHEMATICS AND LANGUAGE

Almost everyone would agree, however, uncomfortably, that sooner or later, as the human population increases in density and at the same time keeps on inventing more powerful and efficient modes of electronic communication, there will emerge a universal language, fluently read and spoken by everyone. There is no way of guessing at what the new language will be like, any more than the early speakers of proto–Indo-Germanic could have guessed ahead at Icelandic or German or Dutch or — the biggest surprise — English. Whatever it turns out to be, there will of course always be regional dialects of the new tongue, but everyone will be able to comprehend, more or less plainly, everyone else, all around the earth, which is surely not the case now, nor has ever been. No one believes this will happen soon, certainly not in the lifetime of the people alive today, maybe not for centuries. But it will come, sooner or later, provided of course that we stay alive as a species, keeping ourselves out from under the hill.

There are indeed some who assert, on reasonable grounds, that the aborginal phonemes of such a universal language already exist, and are ordained to spread everywhere. The trouble is, at the present time, very few of us can speak it or comprehend it, and most of us are blankly unaware of its existence. The universal language of the future, in the view of the tiny minority who now use it for their lives, will be mathematics.

It could be so. Certainly, no other human endeavor can present so powerful an argument for a long survival in the centuries ahead, nor so solid a case for having already influenced and changed, largely for the better, the human condition. Among the sciences, mathematics has advanced more rapidly and at the same time penetrated the human mind more profoundly than any other field. I would include, most conspicuously, physics, for all the showiness of its accomplishments, and even cosmophysics; these disciplines would still be studying Galileo were it not for events that have happened in just the last three centuries in pure mathematics.

The nineteenth-century mathematicians transformed the field so drastically that their work is widely regarded as too advanced to be made accessible to high school students, even university undergraduates. Most of what is called mathematics in the curriculum, in the United States, is essentially that subject as it existed at the end of the eighteenth century.

Ordinary language can be taken as a biological *given;*

we are born with centers and circuits for making words and stringing them along in sentences that make sense to any listener. Mathematics is quite something else, not in our genes, not waiting in the wings of our minds for the proper time to begin speaking numbers. Numbers, their symbols and the ways of manipulating them into the outer spaces of abstraction have to be worked at, *learned.* To be sure, our sort of species has long required an agility with numbers for its plans to succeed and make progress as a social species, but meeting this imperative is not a gift we come by automatically, as we do with speech. The IE root for MATHEMATICS, prophesying the whole future of the enterprise, was *mendh,* meaning learn. Not a root suggesting something natural, lying around in the world waiting to be picked up. On the contrary, a new, ungiven human activity, requiring lots of hard thought and hard work, even possibly, at the end of the day, unattainable. But *mendh,* learning something, also implies something peculiarly pleasurable for the human mind, with cognates carrying the meaning of awake, alert, wise and eager. *Mendh* is also a relative of words meaning to direct the mind, to pay heed to.

In short, we are not born with numbers in our heads, waiting to be put to use. At our beginning, thousands of years ago, all we possessed for computation were the five fingers on each hand; later on, probably, we noticed our toes. Even with these handy counters at hand, it must have taken a very long time, primitive culture after culture, to learn how to manipulate them. We can see fossil traces in words indicating the connection between numbers and finger-counting: the Sanskrit for five is *pantcha*, the Persian for hand is *pentcha;* Russian *piat* is five, *piast* is hand.

Today's clusters of primitive peoples, living in isolation from other cultures, do not have much of a lexicon for numbers. African Bushmen, for example, have words meaning one and two, but beyond that only a word signifying many. Our own putative ancestors must have passed through the same stage of innumeracy before they came upon finger-counting. Some of the words in European languages suggest a memory of that distant defect (as is pointed out by Dantzig in his great book on the evolution of mathematics, *Number, the Language of Science*): the English THRICE and Latin *ter* both have the double meaning of three times and many. Dantzig suggests a similar connection (unattested) between Latin *tres*, three, and *trans*, beyond; also French *très*, very, and *trois*, three.

The permanent dominance of the decimal system of computation is, almost beyond doubt, due to the embedding of finger-counting in almost all cultures. The introduction of symbols for numbers is an event lost in prehistory, probably with its earliest manifestations in the form of orderly scratches and grooves on bones and stones dating back twenty thousand years or more. It was not until recently, only around fifty-five hundred years ago, that systematic methods for writing numerals were invented, and it was only then that any sort of computation became a possibility. Geometry and arithmetic were not really installed in the human mind until the flowering of Greek culture, and then the enterprise would have lagged back during the whole of the first millennium of the present era except for the astonishing inventiveness of the Arab and Hindu mathematicians. These were the minds which put in place the real foundations of what we today call higher mathematics. A flexible, simple numbering system, the positioning of sequential numerals for computation, and the indispensable recognition of zero as a number all came from our relatives to the east. It was only eight centuries ago that these instruments were put to use in Europe, and even then the news was not entirely welcome. Leonardo of Pisa (known best to us by his other name, Fibonacci) introduced zero and began the work of arithmetic with arabic numerals, but the transition to algebra itself took at least two more centuries of argumentation. On one side were the *Abacists*, holding to the traditional reliance on the abacus and similar devices; on the other side the new thinkers, the *Algorists*, possessed of the incontestably more elegant and adaptable system of positional numeration. In some places, algebra was actually illegal and the use of arabic numerals was forbidden in official documents.

Fibonacci did something more than assist at the ushering in of algebra, zero and number theory. He should have been, but was not, lastingly famous for that achievement, but he did another thing. He imagined a pair of rabbits, male and female, inside an enclosure, bearing a similar pair after two months, and then each month another pair is produced, with each pair populating the world of rabbits in the same fashion and at the same rate. Count then the number of rabbit couples, month by month.

The result is the Fibonacci series, a sequence of numbers beginning as 1, 1, 2, 3, 5, 8, 13, 21, 34, 55, 89, 144, 233, 377, 610, 987, 1597, 2584, 4181 etc., each number the sum of the two preceding numbers, which has provided more entertainment for amateur nonmathematicians than any other puzzle I've ever come across. You do not have to be a mathematician to see the pleasure in these numbers, but I believe (and I may be quite wrong about this) that you can catch at least a distinct glimpse of what real mathematicians do, or used to do, with their time.

There are some important aspects of the Fibonacci series to lay out, discovered long ago by others. As the numbers increase, the relationship of each number to the following one begins to approach the irrational number 1.6180339 . . . The number 610, for example, is the fifteenth in the series (F15) and the next up is 987. Divide 987 by 610, you get 1.6180327. Further on, F26 is 121,393, followed by F27, 196,418; divide F27 by F26, you get 1.6180339 . . . , which is as close to the "golden ratio" as you will ever get. Generations of mathematicians have speculated about the significance of this ratio, for it keeps turning up in unexpected places. It is the harmonious proportion of one length to another in the structure of the Parthenon, it describes the relationship of the spirals of seeds going clockwise in a sunflower compared with those going counterclockwise; it can be seen in the arrangement of fronds on a pine cone or chambers in a nautilus shell, and just recently it has turned out to be the basis for the packing of "quasicrystals," the new and puzzling chemical solids formed by combining and then cooling molten aluminum, manganese and other metals. It may, indeed, represent the best way to pack things closely together in nature, when no other way will do, including the packing of pentagons by the mathematician Roger Penrose, known as Penrose tiling.

Anyone with a pocket calculator can find one entertainment after another in the series. For instance, the squares of the Fibonacci numbers are great fun. When you add the squares of any two numbers, 55, say, the tenth in the series (the square is 3025), plus the fifteenth, 610 (the square is 372,100), you get 375,125. The tenth and fifteenth numbers in the series are five numbers apart; the fifth F number is 5. Divide 375,125 by 5, and you get 75,025, which is precisely the twenty-fifth number in the series. Unaccountably to me, this always works when the sum of the two rank numbers is itself odd, 25 as in this case. But when the sum is even, say the tenth plus the sixteenth (55^2 and 987^2), you must subtract the smaller square from the larger. Thus, 987^2 (974,169) minus 55^2 (3025) yields 971,144; divide this by the F numbers representing the sixth in the series, which is 8, and you get 121,393, precisely the twenty-sixth F number in the series.

There is another nice feature, not needing a calculator. The Fibonacci series contains a lovely, half-hidden cyclicity; it repeats itself with unfailing regularity every twenty-four numbers. This reveals itself when you convert each number to a single digit by adding all the digits comprising the number. Thus, 13 becomes 4, 55 becomes 10 becomes 1, 987 is 24 is 6, and so forth. When you do this, the sequence runs as follows:

1, 1, 2, 3, 5, 8, 4, 3, 7, 1, 8, 9 /
8, 8, 7, 6, 4, 1, 5, 6, 2, 8, 1, 9 /
1, 1, 2, 3, 5, 8, 4, 3, 7, 1, 8, 9 /
8, 8, 7, 6, 4, 1, 5, 6, 2, 8, 1, 9, etc.

This works nicely as far out as I've been inclined to take it, which are the heavy numbers of the forty-ninth through the fifty-second in the series. The forty-ninth is 7,778,742,049, which sums to 1. The fiftieth is 12,586,269,025, also 1. The fifty-first is 20,365,011,074, summing to 2. And the fifty-second is 32,951,280,099, or 3. I have no doubt the next numbers will add to 5, 8, 4, 3, 7 and so forth, but I've not tried.

I bring up these shoals of numbers and their repeated cycles, when reduced to single digits, not out of vanity (although I admit to some self-indulgence) but rather the opposite: to disclose that I cannot be a mathematician. I displayed with some pride the list and its cyclicity to a physicist friend, a proper, upper-class mathematician. He looked at it rather casually, then said, "That's quite nice. Now can you prove it?" And, for the life of me, I didn't know what he was asking for. That was, and is, the depth of my ignorance. The cycles were there in the numbers, enough I'd thought, but I had, and still have, no equation to prove they would go on this way forever, nor any notion how to find one.

Et Cetera, Et Cetera

It was the notion of zero, and its polar equivalent infinity, that took the longest time for acceptance, and, once accepted, had the most stimulating effects on the developing science. Zero originated in India, where the word *sunya* in computing meant simply blank or empty, not at all the meaning of nothing at all which it later assumed. *Sunya* was translated by the tenth-century Arabs as *sifr*, meaning empty. The Italians turned *sifr* into *zephirum*, and by the fourteen century the term had become ZERO. The old Arabic *sifr* lived on, however, becoming *cifra* for the German mathematicians, whence CIPHER in English and its retained meaning of zero.

By the sixteenth century, the new arithmetic, together with the rediscovery and development of a sophisticated geometry and algebra, had become solidly established as the basis of mathematical thought, and the modern science was ready to take off.

As an outsider, I cannot pretend to understand the accomplishments of the science. I can only read what some of the professional mathematicians have written, translated by them into plain English for people like me. Not many of the great professionals have done this, but these few have easily convinced me that humankind is on to something altogether new, and wonderful.

Felix Browder and Saunders MacLane, for example, in an essay written twelve years ago, summarized the major events that converted pure mathematics into a totally new branch of science, yielding up relativity and quantum mechanics within just the twentieth century. They concluded, in 1978, that *"mathematics, as the science of significant form, interacts in an ever widening*

Mathematics and Language

way with the whole framework of human thought and practice," and they provide compelling examples of the advances they have in mind.

So, I take it on faith, and rely more than ever on the professional philosopher I've always held in enduring regard. Alfred North Whitehead, back in 1941, wrote the following words about mathematics as a language for the future:

> The notion of the importance of pattern is as old as civilization. Every art is founded on the study of pattern. The cohesion of social systems depends on the maintenance of patterns of behavior, and advances in civilization depend on the fortunate modification of such behavior patterns. . . .
>
> Mathematics is the most powerful technique for the understanding of pattern, and for the analysis of the relation of patterns. Here we reach the fundamental justification for the topic of Plato's lecture [On the Good]. Having regard to the immensity of its subject matter, mathematics, even modern mathematics, is a science in its babyhood. If civilization continues to advance in the next two thousand years, the overwhelming novelty in human thought will be the dominance of mathematical understanding.

The great lesson to be learned from the history of mathematics is not in the events themselves, nor in the immense progress that the science has achieved in the last few centuries. These are highly technical matters,

still comprehensible only within the minority who have
concentrated their minds on the subject in order to use
mathematics for their professional careers. For the rest
of us, mathematically illiterate, speechless, it must be
obvious that something totally new has been introduced
into human thought, and this has happened within a
brief and very recent period of our existence. It needs
remembering, here at the end of the twentieth century
A.D. that this is actually the end of our three hundred
sixtieth century, and the new way of thinking about the
world did not even begin until, at the outside, just thirty
centuries ago, and did not really soar upwards into high
abstraction until three hundred years ago, and is probably still only in its early stage of development. The new
way of thinking should not be attributed to any one of
our provincial cultures. Much of the progress in recent
years was, to be sure, the product of Western industri-
alized societies, but the roots from which today's mathematics emerged lie back in Old Egypt, Old Greece, and
the Hindu and Arab cultures flourishing during the Dark
Ages of the West. Mathematics is, in short, a *human*
achievement, a spectacular instance of human beings
learning a new kind of thought. It should be telling us
over and over again that we are a young species, beginning to grow up, feeling our way along together, free, in
at least this sense, of our genes, *learning*. Whitehead was
right: we could be on our way to a new and universal
language, and a new way of thinking together.

The future holds the promise that our species will be
thinking together in a new way, carrying the abstractions and symbolizations already embedded in today's

language onto a new, higher plane. This does not mean that we will be saying to each other things like "$\sqrt{2}$" or "$\sqrt{-1}$" with quizzical eyebrows lifted, nor will "$\dfrac{1+\sqrt{5}}{2}$" be a commonplace expression of approval for a new building project. We will not be using, as old aphorisms, Gödel's equations, or Fermat's last theorem. But we will be achieving a comprehension of such matters, and others considerably deeper still awaiting the grasp of the mathematicians among us. The extremities of today's physical science, the calculations of the cosmological and particle physicists, will be understood in detail by all reasonably educated citizens of the world.

Easy to say. But still not enough to satisfy the Whitehead prediction. If things go well in the human mind, really well, we will be doing our thinking together with much the same kind of logic that our mathematicians have been writing on their blackboards over the last two centuries, with a statistically better chance of being right about the world and its ways than the fantasies on which most of us have relied over the millennia. We may then, if the thinking goes as well as it might, be making *sense* of the world, even the universe, even our biological and social selves.

This seems to me, as I write, a cold and excessively orderly way for the collective mind of mankind to be working, too cold to think about. Still, I hanker for the shift, even though it lies far beyond my time of living, for it seems to me not just a good wish for the species but an altogether natural process of development, the real beginning of growing up. Or, anyway, an aspect of maturation for our kindred still to come.

The etymology of MATHEMATICS is, looked at closely, a tribute to the language. The modern meaning, given by most dictionaries in one form or another, is the study of patterns, relationships and connections, using rigorously defined literal, numerical and operational symbols. "The science of numbers" is enough for pocket dictionaries, but offers only the surface.

It is as though the language had the hunch, at its very beginning, that such a future for the mind would come into being. The IE root was *mendh*, with the general meaning being simply to learn. The Greeks used the root for *mathema*, a lesson, *mathesis*, desire for learning, *mathanein*, to learn, and *mathematikos*, disposed to learn. Not necessarily about numbers. Although the Greeks had numbers, arithmetic and geometry, these had their own special terms. Mathematics was the word for acquiring new information, learning about the world.

The Greek *mathematikos* is cognate with Sanskrit *medha*, wisdom, and Avestan *mazda*, memory, the ultimate sources of English MIND. Words based on *mendh* turned up in Old Germanic as *muntar*, eager, awake, in Old Slavic as *modru*, wise, and (perhaps most prophetically) in Old Icelandic as *munda*, with the meaning of striving for, directing the mind toward.

The numbers came later, the symbols later still, and nobody knows what mathematics is in for in the centuries ahead. But there is the certainty that the root will still hold, that the inner meaning of the term will be the same, to learn a new thing.

39

NUMB, NUMBER, NIMBLE etc.

Sometimes the language displays a sense of humor all its own. The Indo-Europeans seem to have had very little arithmetic, and no way to write numbers that we know of, but they did indeed have some names for numbers. *Dwo* was two, *trei* was three, *kwetwer* four, *penkwe* five, *swek* six, *septm* seven, *okto* eight, *newn* nine, *dekm* ten. But there is no known IE root for our word NUMBER except *nem*, which for the Indo-Europeans carried only the meaning of something taken, seized or allotted — close enough to the notion of numbering, I suppose, but not really NUMBER. That word came later, in descendant languages: perhaps, as AHD suggests, by way of a suffixed form *nom-ess*, thence into Latin as *numerus*, NUMBER.

But some of the other cognates derived from *nem*, and therefore hanging together in our language, tell how we may be feeling about calculating. NUMB, for one, a direct cognate, probably derived from the sense of being seized, taken. We made a comparable leap with the cognates of the IE root *ster*, meaning stiff, which entered Latin as *torpere*, to stiffen, and emerged in German as *sterben*, to die, and in English as TORPID, TORPOR and, bless the language, TORPEDO, first the electric fish and finally the weapon.

NIMBLE comes from *nem*, by way of Germanic and Old English *naemel*, quick to seize. Greek had *nomos*, a portion, also the customs of a culture, leading to our ASTRONOMY, the ways of the heavens, and ANOMIE, no way.

My favorite cognate from *nem* is NEMESIS, out of Greek *nemein*, to allot, also to avenge. Whether capitalized as Nemesis, the goddess of retribution, or ordinary nemesis, the act of justice, it means one's number is, as we say, up.

40

——

TESTAMENT, THIRD PARTY,
GAIA etc.

I contain, somewhere in storage files in one attic room or another of my brain, a very large amount of information about the world and nature, much of it filed under "science," with subfiles for the various categories of research that have consumed most of my time and energy over the fifty-something years spent in laboratories and scientific libraries (also offices, but I doubt I filed the offices anywhere). Trouble is, I can't retrieve the items I need in any systematic way; I'm not even sure beforehand that what I need is there, and more often than not I become engaged in acerbic arguments with myself over whether I really *need* this or that item. The first item, just arrived for pondering on a late, gray afternoon, following a session with the family lawyer, is the ponderous phrase LAST WILL and TESTAMENT. WILL is simple enough, an honest word meaning just what it says, from IE *wel*, to wish, to live WELL, with some overly hopeful cognates like GALA and GALLANT, even WEALTH, nice to have in mind after signing a LAST WILL. But LAST is ambiguous, meaning the latest thing in other contexts, something in high fashion; sometimes a highly improbable occasion: "the LAST thing I would have imagined"; finally the very LAST, the LAST breath, "we've seen the LAST of him." TESTAMENT is the hardest of the words, needing looking up, something quite odd about that word. Look it up.

The IE root of TESTAMENT is *trei*, meaning three, sure enough. Sanskrit *tri*, Greek *trias*, Germanic *thrifiz*, Persian *si*, Slavic *trojc*, all three. Why then TESTAMENT?

Lurking inside TESTAMENT (the dictionary: "a statement of belief or conviction, credo") is another word with another meaning: a third person, a witness, Latin *testis*, a witness standing by. Good thing, too, for if you are of two minds about the larger meaning of human existence, as I am, it may be useful to recruit a third party.

Accordingly, I shall do just that, enlisting my own witness from somewhere (I think) in the folds of my right hemisphere, to overrule at the outset one of my minds, the one who keeps asserting that the place is arranged at random, purposelessly, planlessly, without any meaning at all. With that one silenced, for the time anyway, I and my witness, my inner inhibitor and editor, can proceed.

I believe, first of all, that the earth is a living organism, of greater size but probably no more complexity than any other attested biological organism, including our own human selves. We, for our part, are the equivalent of cells within the body of that creature, or perhaps something rather less independent, organelles inside proper cells. The whole thing breathes, metabolizes, adjusts its working parts (including us) automatically, autonomically, to changes within its internal environment. Also its external environment, remembering meteorite collisions, sunspots, tilting of the orbital axis, cosmic rays and the like. In any case, the surest, unmistakable evidence of coherent life, all of a piece, is its astonishing skill in maintaining the stability and equilibrium of the constituents of its atmosphere, most spectacularly the fixed levels of oxygen and, *pace* us, CO_2, the pH and salinity of its oceans, the diversity and developmental novelty of its "five kingdoms" of live components, the vast wiring diagram that maintains the interconnectedness and interdependence of all its numberless parts, and the ultimate product of the life: more and more information. It is the Gaia hypothesis proposed in 1973 by Lovelock and Margulis, the notion that the earth is a living, self-regulating being.

I think I have believed something like this about the earth for many years, but now I take it into full consciousness as a central, plain fact of life, attested as it now is by the hard data assembled by Lovelock in recent years.

A life of this kind, a sort of immense round organism covering every area of surface and extending out into the upper reaches of its own atmosphere, could only come into existence and remain there if provided with a constant source of energy and an unfillable sink to assure the steady flow, in and away, of that energy. This,

as Morowitz pointed out in a small, lovely book fifteen
years ago, is thanks entirely to the sun and the dynamical, nonequilibrium steady state, energy flowing to our
surface and out to the sink of space, a permanent arrangement from our point of view even though the inevitable decay some billions of years out will stop
everything (but by that time, I like to think, we and the
rest of life will long since have lodged our collective
selves [self] elsewhere).

This brings me to an answer to the heaviest of all the
criticisms of the Lovelock-Margulis Gaia idea. If the
earth is *coherently* alive, how can it be fitted into our
standing criterion for the defining of an organism: reproduction. The answer is, of course, stick around and
watch. We are already at it, still only in the earliest
stages, preparing the seeds and their pods for distribu-
tion on solar winds, not just in our suburban solar system but out into the galaxy and away. That is what we
are doing, with the same awareness of pleasure and excitement that accompanies that act of reproduction at
every level in biology, enraptured by the mechanics of
space travel without a thought to its end result, the rep-
lication of life abroad.

I wrote, back a bit, that the human species might
rank in the scale of living parts as something analogous
to a cell, then I added, in surrogate modesty, that we
might do better as an analogy to an organelle, as individuals I meant. As a collective species, however, we
rank much higher, grander than a single cell, something
more at the level of a living tissue. This status I attribute
to two of our biological endowments: the complexity and

size of our brains, and the genetically determined nature
of our social living. First, our brain. We are, so far as
we know, unique among the living components of the
earth for having a brain capable not only of awareness
and what we call consciousness (I happen to believe that
a great many other animals, including my cat and all
the social insects, possess the same sort of awareness),
but we do something more than this. We record the details of our past experience and make compulsive
guesses about our future (much as I am engaged in at
the moment). More than this, and here is our uniquely
distinguishing feature, we *talk* to each other about these
things. In short, we are unique because of language. But
this alone would not be enough to set us at our proper
station in nature. The really important, far and away
most important thing about human beings is human society. We are, with an intensity and lifelong commitment
beyond any other species on the planet, a biologically,
mandatorily, ineluctably social animal. We could never
survive as single, separate individuals. We have the capacity to think together as we talk, and under ideal circumstances we can generate thoughts of a magnitude
beyond the comprehension of any single one of us. A
conspicuous example of this trait is language itself, so
strange and new a phenomenon as to pass all under-
standing. And, because of language, a literature, a body
of art, pure mathematics, a feeling for music (the
strangest and thus far the best of our achievements, in
my view), and, when we do not in folly suppress it, a
deep affection for each other.

I said, under *ideal* circumstances, which is an evasive

way of saying we haven't done these things to our capacity, not yet.

But look at us, and where we came from, and consider how new we are to the earth, and how young. We have existed as real human beings, by every definition we make for ourselves, for a mere few thousand years, an almost undetectable flash of time, no time at all in geological time-spans. Here in the last years of our own twentieth century, we could, of course, become extinct at any time, but surely not because of any lack of capacity to compete with other species, not because of Neanderthal befuddlement. If we are to become extinct, it will be our own clever, ingenious handiwork.

But, for some encouragement, take a glance at what we have already done with a few words in just our own branch of the language. There was an ancient root, *bheu*, which contained the notion of growing into existence, with BE and BEING as part of our inheritance. It came into early Greek as *phuein*, to bring forth and make grow, becoming *phusis*, live nature itself, then *phutos*, a plant. Later, English took it for PHYSICS, as Aristotle had used *ta physika* for his speculations on natural science.

The original notion of being and growing, embedded inside *bheu* from the beginning, modified the root in other ways for later, still more practical metaphors. The necessities of living and preparing together produced our words BE and BEING. FUTURE, from the same root, came by way of Latin *futurus*, "that is to be" (also, to make sure of the prediction, *fiat*, let it be, for our FIAT). Old Norse used *bua*, to live and prepare, for words that we took on as BONDAGE, HUSBAND (with BOND as a closely related obligation). Germanic provided *buthla* for our BUILD and BUILDING. Middle Dutch had *bodel* for property and wealth, from which in an off moment we made BOODLE.

And at last, to take the language back to the sensations that lay beneath the first root, *bheu* is now attested as the source of Old English *beam*, a tree, our word BEAM, and Middle Dutch *boom*, also a tree, leaving us only the BOOM of a sailing vessel.

Another word filled with allusions to conditions in the peculiar human existence, and telling us many things about our expectations of ourselves, was the IE root *gen*, with the meaning to give birth, beget. The derivatives deal with aspects of family life, social living in groups ranging from tribes to nation states, and with our attitudes and behavior toward each other as individuals and abstractions. Some of these are the most encouraging words in speech; using this root the language seems to have turned its face to us and revealed its ambitions for what we might become. The variant *gna* entered Latin as *praegnas*, PREGNANT, and when a suffix *-sko* was added, out came new words from Latin *gnasci*: NATURE in all its meanings, including good-natured, NATIVE, NATAL and, placing us forever in harm's way, NATION. The Germanic derivatives became KIN and KINDRED as the same word, and KIND became the other kind of KIND, with KINDNESS. The Latin derivative *gens*, signifying only a race or clan, and the French *gens*, meaning people at large, provided from their inner senses *gentil* and *gentihomme*, and one of our best words,

GENTLE. Along with words connected to birth, GENER-
ATION, GENITAL, GENEALOGY and GENETIC, came
words telling what being born might mean: GENIUS, GE-
NIAL, INGENIOUS, BENIGN, and, no surprise here, GEN-
EROUS.

We are still young, as a species, still learning our way
round the world, and now at a dangerous age, something
like late childhood or early adolescence, prone to folly
for the centuries just ahead. Already we show signs of
getting beyond ourselves, as we say of children, and in
the organization of our affairs as nation states we have
a long record of fecklessness. For all our regard for each
other close at hand, in families and groups of friends,
when we assemble ourselves in crowds and try to think
together in excitement, we lose a part of our minds and
language, and turn murderous. I do not understand the
mechanism of this disorder, and I can only hope that we
will outgrow it. We have known about it for a long time;
our word THREAT came from Latin *trudere*, into Old
English as *threat*, "a crowd or crush of people."

What we need, for the years ahead, more than anything else, is time, time to grow up, time to learn.

Learning, come to think of it, is really what we are
best of all at. Language is a wonder, of course, but
learning is what language allows us to do, and learning
is what we need most as a species. Science is part of this.
From my viewpoint, professionally prejudiced as it is,
science is a very important part at this stage, but not yet
the most important. There are a great many things to
learn about ourselves, and about the earth, and about

our obligations to the earth and to each other, for which we will not have our instructions from science alone, maybe not from science at all. I suspect we will pick up information of the sort needed for a future from changes in our feelings about ourselves in very large numbers, and about the earth as a very large, and by and large good-natured (although in our terms also very tough) creature.

One thing that eludes me, always has and likely always will. If the earth is what I think it is, an immense being, intact and coherent, does it have a mind? If it does, what is it thinking? We like to tell each other these days, in our hubris, that we are the thinking part, the earth's awareness of itself; without us and our marvelous brains, even the universe would not exist — we form it and all the particles of its structure, and without us on the scene the whole affair would pop off in the old random disorder. I believe only a little of this, to the extent that whatever awareness we manage to achieve comes automatically into the earth's reach. But I believe another thing, somewhat larger. The earth consists of a multitude, a near-infinity of living species, all engaged in some kind of thought. Moths, for instance, do their kind of thinking; they have receptors for the ultrasound probes of bats, and swerve to one side or the other or drop to the ground if the bat is at a distance safe enough for that maneuver, but if the bat is close by, a meter or so away, and escape is nearly impossible, the moth does some very hard, quick thinking and switches chaos on in its brain. The result is a series of wild, unpredictable daring movements, and because of these an occasional lucky moth escapes.

Given brains all over the place, all engaged in thought — some of these to be sure very small thoughts, but all interacting and interconnected at least in the sense that the separate termites in a twenty-foot-tall termite hill are interconnected — and given the living mass of the earth and its atmosphere, including the swamps and the waters under the earth, there must be something like a mind at work, adrift somewhere around or over or within the mass.

My scientist friends will not be liking this notion, although I shouldn't think they would object to the less grand view that *any* electronically monitored system of living agents in close connection and communication with each other, sooner or later, when the mass of agents becomes large enough and dense enough, might begin to emit signals indicating coherence and moments of synchrony. Even so, my friends will object to the term *mind*, worrying that I am proposing something mystical, a governor of the earth's affairs, a Presence, something *in charge*, issuing orders to this part or that, running the place.

Not a bit of it, or maybe only a little bit; my fantasy is of a different nature. It is merely there, an immense collective thought, spread everywhere, unconcerned with the details. It is, if it exists, the *result* of the earth's life, not at all the cause. What does it do, this mind of my imagining, if it does not operate the machine? It contemplates, that's what it does, is my answer.

Testament, Third Party, Gaia etc.

No big deal, I tell my scientist friends; not to worry. It hasn't noticed you yet in any case. And anyway, if It has a preoccupation with any part of Itself in particular, this would likely be, as Haldane once remarked, all the various and multitudinous beetles.

Sources

American Heritage Dictionary. Boston: Houghton Mifflin, 1973.

American Heritage Dictionary. Boston: Houghton Mifflin, 1981.

Barnhart, R. K., ed. *Barnhart Dictionary of Etymology*. New York: H. W. Wilson Co., 1988.

Bickerton, D. *Roots of Language*. Ann Arbor: Karoma Publishers, 1981.

Encyclopaedia Britannica. New York: Encyclopaedia Britannica Co., 1910.

Greenough, J. B., and Kittredge, G. L. *Words and Their Ways in English Speech*. Boston: Beacon Paperback. 1962.

Johnson, Samuel. *A Dictionary of the English Language*, 1755. London: J. S. Pratt edition, 1847.

Liddell and Scott. *Greek-English Lexicon*. Oxford: Oxford University Press, 1987.

Lovelock, James E. *The Ages of Gaia*. New York: Norton, 1988.

Lovelock, J. E., and Margulis, L. "Atmospheric homeostasis

by and for the biosphere: The Gaia hypothesis." *Tellus*, 26 (1973):2.

Morowitz, Harold. *Energy Flow in Biology*. New York: Academic Press, 1968.

Onions, C. T., ed. *The Oxford Dictionary of English Etymology*. Oxford: Oxford University Press, 1983.

Oxford English Dictionary. Oxford: Oxford University Press, 1978 edition.

Partridge, Eric. *Origins: A Short Etymological Dictionary of Modern English*. New York: Greenwich House, 1983.

Pokorny, Julius. *Indogermanisches Etymologisches Wörterbuch*. Bern: A. Francke AG Verlag, 1959.

Shipley, J. T. *Dictionary of Word Origins*. Totowon, N.J.: Littlefield, Adams & Co., 1970.

Simpson, D. P. *Cassell's Latin Dictionary*. New York: Macmillan, 1968.

Skeat, W. W. *Concise Etymological Dictionary of the English Language* (1882). Oxford: Capricorn Edition, 1963 edition.

Weekley, Ernest. *An Etymological Dictionary of Modern English*. New York: Dover, 1967.

White, Randall. *Dark Caves, Bright Visions: Life In Ice Age Europe*. New York: American Museum of Natural History and W. W. Norton & Co., Inc., 1986.

Index of
English Words

189

Index

Index

Index

Index

Index